Write Like Hemingway

E. J. Gleason

Write Like Hemingway

13-Digit ISBN: 978-1-60433-887-4
10-Digit ISBN: 1-60433-887-3

This book may be ordered by mail from the publisher. Please include $5.99 for postage and handling. Please support your local bookseller first! Books published by Cider Mill Press Book Publishers are available at special discounts for bulk purchases in the United States by corporations, institutions, and other organizations. For more information, please contact the publisher.

Cider Mill Press Book Publishers
"Where good books are ready for press"
PO Box 454
12 Spring Street
Kennebunkport, Maine 04046
Visit us online!
cidermillpress.com

Back cover image © Robert Capa/Magnum Photos
Typography: Benton Sans, FreightText Pro, Sunflower,
Zai Consul Polish Typewriter

Printed in the United States of America
1 2 3 4 5 6 7 8 9
First Edition

Find Your Voice, Discover Your Style

Write Like Hemingway

10 Rules That Guided a Nobel Laureate

E. J. Gleason

Contents

"If I started to wait for moments of inspiration, I would never finish a book. Inspiration for me comes from a regular effort."

— Mario Vargas Llosa, from *Writers At Work: The Paris Review Interviews*

Introduction

"I always worked until I had something done and I always stopped when I knew what was going to happen next. That way I could be sure of going on the next day."

— From *A Moveable Feast*

What would it be like to write with the clarity, precision, and insight of someone whose writing style is an explicit indication of authorship? Ernest Hemingway is one of few writers who enjoys such a distinction. And the characteristics of his style—simple, sincere, and insightful—make generation after generation of aspiring authors and lovers of literature feel that reading his prose is imperative. Moreover, Hemingway's way of using the basic units of language presents itself as an appealing model for anyone so inclined to "write like the master." But the question begged is: How did he learn to write like this?

Hemingway's passion—to live a spirited life and to record how he lived it—was boundless. Against his parents' wishes, he decided not to attend college (he could have studied at either Oberlin College or the University of Illinois), opting instead for a life of adventure. In 1917, right out of high school, he accepted a position as a newspaper reporter at the *Kansas City Star*.

Hemingway had family connections to the ownership of the *Star*, meaning he did not have to interview for his job as a reporter, or beat out another upstart. In spite of this leg up, and the considerable amount of writing he did at Oak Park High School in Illinois, Hemingway still worried that he might be critically deficient in his knowledge of what constituted "correct" English usage. In his first week of doing police and emergency-room reports for the *Star*, assistant city editor C. G. "Pete" Wellington issued him bullet points of proper usage entitled "The Star Copy Style," a guide compiled over time by veteran *Star* staffers. The chief architect of the guide sheet was the gruff, enigmatic, and legendary editor Thomas W. Johnston Jr. Johnston died just prior to Hemingway's arrival in Kansas City, but his influence on the newspaper's staff reverberated for decades (see page 13). Flawed though the document was—category overlap was a particular issue, as were inflexible and obsolete strictures and proscriptions that were absolutely erroneous—it gave Hemingway all sorts of linguistic matters to contemplate, and alerted him to the discipline required of a professional. Later in his life, reflecting on the best writing advice he'd received in his youth, Hemingway said that the admonitions in the style sheet were "the best rules I ever learned in the business of writing."

Seven months after joining the newspaper's staff, however, Hemingway was desperate to witness and experience action close to the European war front. So he traveled to New York City and signed on with the Red Cross Ambulance Service. Assigned to an Italian ambulance squadron that constantly had to dodge German mortar rounds while rescuing the wounded, Hemingway found the action he craved. Though he was wounded severely during his time on the frontlines, Hemingway's overall experience was incredibly positive, and he began to store the experiences that he would later mine in his fiction.

Hemingway had the great advantage of knowing precisely what he wanted to do for a career early in his life. Knowing what was expected of him in that career only furthered that advantage. Before he turned 26, he'd not only found a literary voice with which he was comfortable, he'd also developed a writing style that would, in short time, redirect how American fiction would be rendered thereafter.

Hemingway had good writing teachers in high school—including one who set up her classroom like a working newspaper office—but the majority of what Hemingway learned about matters of English usage was what he absorbed from the prose of Rudyard Kipling, Ring Lardner, and the English classic novelists. Lardner, because he was a sports columnist and writer of short stories with a fondness for tough, colloquial speech, made a particularly large impression on the young Hemingway, as one sees in Hemingway's coverage of sporting events for his high school newspaper. The *Kansas City Star* style guide augmented those early instincts by giving a form to what had been general rules of thumb, allowing Hemingway to move among his peers at the *Star* with a feeling of professional adequacy.

The theme of the style guide is evident from the first entry: "Use short sentences. Use short first paragraphs. Use vigorous English. Be positive, not negative." The first two dicta are clear, and they became the central aims of Hemingway's writing: compress wherever possible; waste no words. While "vigorous English" is open to interpretation, if it is intended to denote words characteristically associated with the athletic arena, then Hemingway would be a primary writer to go to for examples. Advising writers to "Be positive, not negative" is also too vague to judge its effect on Hemingway. If being positive translates into writing forcefully and confidently, then we can see that it applied to Hemingway in every aspect, and it is doubtful that any writer's prose is more consistently forceful than Hemingway's.

Aspiring writers typically lack the self-confidence and self-discipline to follow the dictum laid down by the Roman rhetorician Horace: "*nulla dies sine linea,*" which translates to "never a day without a line." While this examination of Hemingway's work will provide some helpful precepts, they will not matter one whit if you never get around to sitting at a desk and writing, day after day. That, as much as any lesson gleaned from the *Kansas City Star's* style guide, is what enabled Hemingway to attain the mastery of language that lifted "The Snows of Kilimanjaro," *The Old Man and the Sea*, and *The Sun Also Rises* into the American canon.

For those who can muster the enthusiasm needed to make this commitment, *Write Like Hemingway* is as much a promise as it is an invitation. And not just for aspiring writers of fiction. Whether one's purpose is to invent a character and a plot, explain a process, describe a phenomenon, or argue an issue, the principles exhibited in Hemingway's writing are applicable across all disciplines and discourses.

While it is common for novices to look to the work of the greats in order to get their bearing, the unique character of Hemingway's writing makes this particular form of admiration more common with him than with any other literary legend. Joan Didion and Hunter S. Thompson, highly original and great writers in their own right, admitted to typing out Hemingway's novels during their formative years, trying to drill Papa's muscular rhythms into their heads.

It is this feature of Hemingway's writing—the potential for emulation—that I will explore here. By identifying the features of Hemingway's writing and examining how he learned and developed them, it is possible for a writer to follow the trail he blazed. Embedded in each of his sentences is a thorough lesson in how to write well, and, if we dig into that "plainspeak prose," we will come up with more than enough compositional strategies to fire your creative impulse, dear reader.

Imitation is an entry point, and its ability to provide the beginner with a direction and momentum is powerful. But it cannot be the endgame. In order to produce revolutionary work, one will have to move beyond their idols, into the self. When perfecting the imitation becomes the terminal goal of the learner, the value in any artistic field is limited. As such, the inclination toward imitation should eventually give way to a pursuit of the personalized.

As celebrated as Hemingway's severely unadorned style is, it has also frequently been the object of parody. This is inevitable with distinctive literary styles, as the Gothic tales of Edgar Allan Poe, the stream-of-consciousness flights of James Joyce, and the cryptic proclamations of Emily Dickinson have each been the frequent target of such caricatures. It could be argued that parody is an even higher form of flattery than imitation, for it is a recognition that one has managed to produce something without precedent, which is different and yet immediately recognizable.

As with any form of humor, the stakes get higher with the passage of time, and, inevitably, the clever parodies of Hemingway's work—which are possible only if there is a healthy respect for the source material—evolved into outright lampoons, less sophisticated critiques that sought only to savage Hemingway's stylistic achievement. The author was long dead when groups of Hemingway-haters began inviting people to submit their worst approximations of his truncated dialogue and stringing together of multiple independent clauses. But, as with any critical endeavor, the artistic shortcomings exposed are more those of the attacker than the attacked.

The challenge is to identify, appropriate, and practice the skills inherent in Hemingway's prose. Hemingway's life experiences cannot be replicated. But the muscular mannerisms of the language that deliver the essence of those experiences is. With that reality in mind, perhaps *Write [Something] Like Hemingway* might better describe the purpose of this book. Ultimately, we are searching for ways to superimpose our experience over his. Think of the purpose of each chapter as pinning the peculiarities of a particular stylistic component to a corkboard and devising a way of re-forming and combining them to reveal a product that is more yours than his.

The scholarship on Hemingway since his death seems in agreement that without the discipline imposed on the young reporter at *The Kansas City Star*—without the impact of the Copy Style specifically—a very different writing style likely would have emerged than the one associated with the Hemingway we know. Certainly, with our interest in the multiple factors that affected his conception of effective writing, much more needs to be said about those 110 precepts, the substance of which Hemingway never in his lifetime ceased to celebrate for the rules and regimen they provided at a make-or-break point in his career. Independent of their role in shaping Hemingway's style, we might also consider what importance those strictures have for writers today in search of a stylistic foundation.

Of 'Star Style,' its creator ... and a reporter named Ernest

From the September 14, 1980, issue of *The Kansas City Star*

The sinking of the Lusitania received an exceptional play in *The Star*. A two-column headline announced the tragedy, the first of many in the next few years. The European powers plunged deeper into war, drawing the United States inexorably toward the trenches, which already snaked across the fields of eastern France.

Yet the war, in its first years, seemed distant in Kansas City. *The Star* supplied readers twice a day with details of the expanding conflict but, on the whole, it still emphasized local news. Reporters, as they would be for the next 60 years, bent over their typewriters, which then were attached to oaken tables in the cavernous city room. The staff rotated as *The Star* finished its run and the night staff of "*The Morning Kansas City Star*," *The Times*, came to work. Almost to a man, the reporters wore caps and hats. Celluloid collars pinched their necks.

But change was in the air. And into the midst of *The Star* staff in late 1917, came a youth who, when he could get away with it, wore a red and black checkered hunting shirt to work. Old timers frowned on such dress.

But the young reporter worked outside the office most of the time. His name was Ernest Hemingway.

Years later scholars would come to Kansas City to investigate Hemingway's tenure at *The Star*, which lasted from October 1917 to April 1918. *The Star* period fascinated Hemingway students because his lean, sparse writing style, basically *Star* style, led him to become one of the most acclaimed writers of the 20th century, winner of the 1954 Nobel Prize for Literature and a legend as a man, warrior, womanizer, and drinker.

The scholars would ask for the library's clippings on Hemingway and C.G. "Pete" Wellington, the assistant city editor of *The Star* in 1917. Hemingway credited Wellington with changing his verbose high school writing style into clear, provocative English. The scholars also requested "The Star Copy Style" sheet, a single, galley-size page, which contained the 110 rules governing *Star* prose. Hemingway later would recall the sheet as something "they gave you to study when you went to work and after that you were just as responsible for having learned it as after you've had the articles of war read to you."

Some researchers would pour over *The Star* of those times on microfilm, failing to turn up what they wanted badly, a story bearing Hemingway's byline or initials. Such stories did not exist. Stories were not identified with bylines; initials were only rarely used. The microfilm signaled the last stop for the scholars. But they usually found where Hemingway lived when he worked at the paper, a rooming house at 3526 Agnes.

Over the years only a few asked for anything more—such as the file on Thomas W. Johnston Jr.

Johnston, known as T.W., Tommy to intimates and "Icicle" to reporters who felt the frost of his glare, remained in the shadows even of *The Star*, a memory quickly forgotten. Quite simply, his work transcended his personality.

Johnston died May 18, 1917, at 54, in a house at Westport and Main. His death notice covered almost all of Page 2 of *The Star* the next day. The following day, Johnston's name ran at the top of the lead editorial. Those stories weren't filed in Johnston's lean library envelope. It contained only recollections of the man written 30 to 40 years after his death.

Yet Johnston gave *The Star* its "magical quality." Johnston, more than any other, "contributed largely to the physical style and established taste of *The Star*." Johnston wrote the "Copy Style" sheet. Wellington, Hemingway's teacher and keeper of the style sheet in 1917, provided the link to Johnston. Although the two men probably never met, that link, once forged, endured. In the early 1960s, young *Star* reporters, between assignments, could be seen studying the rules, by then expanded into a small book. One of those cubs would recall later that he studied the rules more intensely than he had *The Marine's Guidebook* two years earlier as a shaved-head recruit.

As a man, Johnston proved an enigma, floating wraith-like in and out of *Star* documents. He appeared several times, his large, bold handwriting signing, along with Nelson in 1901, the agreement by which Nelson bought *The Times*. Later. He attended meetings of The Kansas City Star Co., a Nelson contrivance to block some lawsuits against the paper in the early part of the century. Again, his signatures appeared on the minutes of The Kansas City Star Building and Investment Co., through which Nelson bought the land at 18th and Grand for $7,500 so he could erect the present home of *The Star*, and on documents of the N-K Land Co., a Nelson-Irwin Kirkwood venture used to buy land for Nelson's home, Oak Hall. Johnston's Attendance at those meeting was attended to by his signature, but his presence was marked by his utter lack of communication at the meetings.

Probably his thoughts concentrated on *The Star*. He served as managing editor 17 years until his twice-daily trips to one of the 35 saloons surrounding *The Star* became too consuming. Nelson reluctantly replaced him with Ralph Stout in 1910, naming Johnston associate editor. Finally, in 1913, Johnston was out all together, an alcoholic.

But not before *The Star* did something unique. The lead editorial on April 11 that year announced Johnston's departure. The Editorial told the story euphemistically. It marked probably the only time in the history of the paper that a staffer leaving the paper received such a standing in its columns. It read:

"It is with the keenest regret that *The Star* announces the retirement from its staff of Thomas W. Johnston, associate editor, after 26 years of brilliant service. His health, which has been such as to make the regular duties of his position irksome, has impelled him to the decision to withdraw from the newspaper world. In reluctantly acquiescing in this determination, *The Star* cannot forbear expression of its admiration of the unique part taken by Mr. Johnston in building up this newspaper. His discriminating intelligence, rare taste and balanced judgement were in evidence in everything he did ... There was no subject he touched he did not illuminate. His style was himself. He was marvelously adaptable to all moods from flaming indignation to the most delicate badinage. Never in his career was he guilty of a dull line or one that fell short of exquisite taste."

Born in Youngstown, Ohio, Johnston came to *The Star* as managing editor in 1887 when the circulation was 20,000. When he retired, the circulation of the morning and evening editions combined was 435,000. Not a prolific writer himself, but one who could sense the touch of greatness in others, Johnston recruited, among others, William Allen White, Stout, Sumner Blossom (later editor of Collier-Cowles) and Courtney Riley Cooper. With his face usually stern and set, rarely smiling, Johnston was a tall man who carried himself with an almost military erectness. "Unbending" was the description. Nelson told Theodore Roosevelt that Johnston more than any other man helped him build *The Star*.

"Serious" described Johnston's attitude toward *The Star*. When the *Topeka Capital* allowed the Rev. Charles M. Sheldon, author of the widely read book *In His Steps*, to edit that paper for a week as he thought Jesus would have, a group of Kansas City matrons rushed to *The Star*, according Nelson. They described to the colonel what a great thing it would be if he let his paper, the most influential daily in the Southwest, carry out the same experiment. Nelson, at a loss for words (a rare state for him), called Johnston. The chairman of the delegation painted the project in glowing colors. Johnston listened silently, his eyes growing colder and colder. Finally, when it was his turn to speak, he said simply:

"Ladies, *The Star* is not a plaything." The interview was over.

Johnston gave similar consideration to the English language. He insisted "that everything which went into the paper be written in clean English and nothing go in that violated the canons of good taste." A *Star* reporter recalled "whenever one of these cardinal principles of his were violated, he had a way of correcting the error which usually prevented its reparation. Instead of saying, 'This is wrong,' he went to the bottom of the matter and said why it was wrong."

The "Copy Style" sheet was a bible, containing eminently practical rules. Among them:

"Never use old slang. Such words as *stunt*, *cut out*, *got his goat*, *come across*, *sit up and take notice*, *put one over*, have no use after their use has become common. Slang to be enjoyable must be fresh.

"Eliminate ever superfluous word as *Funeral services will be at 2 o'clock Tuesday*, not *The funeral services will be held at the hour of 2 o'clock Tuesday*. Avoid the use of adjectives, especially such extravagant ones as *splendid*, *gorgeous*, *grand*, *magnificent*, *etc*.

"Don't say, *He had his leg cut off in an accident*. He wouldn't have had it done for anything.

"*He was eager to go*, not *anxious to go*. You are anxious about a friend who is ill.

"*He died of heart disease*, not *heart failure*—everybody dies of heart failure."

What Johnston codified was a practical, no-nonsense approach to writing. The rules "made extremely good sense," Hemingway recalled in 1952. Yet Johnston had another quality, one that Wellington luckily had, too. With his honest thoroughness and love of the language, Johnston's (and Peter Wellington's) attitude instilled a sense of greatness into a group of young men eager to believe themselves great.

Johnston encouraged his reporters to write with absolute freedom, unhampered save by the truth as they saw it. The result was exceptional newspaper writing in a day when some reporters on other papers made up stories with small regard to the truth, caring little for the craft of writing. For Nelson, the freedom had an added bonus—staff loyalty. Despite their meager wages, a *Star* man cherished his creative freedom. It is little wonder so many of them would develop into smooth storytellers later at other papers across the nation, in the writers' wings of Hollywood studios, and at the major magazines. One *Star* man, long before journalists would be called the "new elite," described working for *The Star*:

"It made us feverish. It sent us along the street, day after day, and year after year ... hoping that streetcars might crash, that murder would rise out of the gutter ... so that I could be on hand to cover the story. It made eternal cubs of us with interest never lagging. We had honor to maintain, prestige to defend, we had constant competition, not from other papers but from our fellow reporters. We had contests among ourselves for the honor of getting more news into the paper than other men ... Reporters must be horror-stricken at any failure in civic pride. They must cheer new development, applaud the man who built his own house, revere the Chamber of Commerce, invoke eternal wrath upon him who doubted the Kansas City spirit. We must think of *The Star* in off hours and show up for work whenever necessary, without extra pay. After all, what was money? Something transitory. But the fame of being a *Star* man would last forever. And we believed it."

Johnston's concept of a newspaper still prevailed in the fall of 1917 when Ernest Hemingway came to *The Star*. He was a big, energetic, round-faced boy of 18 with limitless energy and a desire to be in the thick of the action whether a shooting scrape or chasing ambulances. Hemingway worked at the paper for seven months. In late April 1918, he and Ted Brumback, another *Star* reporter, joined an ambulance unit in Italy. Except for the first two weeks of his employment, when he was mistaken by the rest of the staff for the extremely youthful but brilliant drama critic occupying a read desk, an error even the city editor seemed to share, Hemingway was on the run. Twenty years later Hemingway remembered those days in Kansas City, "how Southwest boulevard slanted and how [I] lay under a Ford while detectives shot two internal revenue agents and how you could sleep in the pressroom bathtub if your legs articulated properly and how when the fog came up in the fall, you could see Hospital hill pushing up, almost smelling its antiseptic concord of odors." But most of all in those later years, Hemingway would remember the style sheet and its core admonition: "Use short sentences. Use short first paragraphs. Use vigorous English. Be positive, not negative."

"Those were the best rules I ever learned for the business of writing," Hemingway said in 1940. "I've never forgotten them. No man with any talent, who feels and writes truly about the thing he is trying to say, can fail to write well if he abides with them."

Of all the men Hemingway met in his brief stay at *The Star*, it was Lionel Calhoun Moise who influenced him the most. Moise might have served as a prototype for the Hemingway tough guy. A big, broad-shouldered man, Moise had become a legend in the city room by the time he was 28 and Hemingway met him, a drinker, nomad reporter, and a man who liked to beat up his women. "He was a big, brutal son-of-a-bitch," recalled Emmet Crozier, the playwright who was on *The Star*'s sports staff at the time. Hemingway dogged Moise's steps, listening to his theories about tying paragraphs together so they couldn't be cut; that pure, objective writing is the only form of storytelling; and lamenting "the regrettable indication of a great nation's literary taste when it chooses a national anthem beginning with the words 'Oh, say.'" Moises set attitudes in Hemingway which later became vital to the man: the need to experience what he wrote about and the use of a minimum of description. Action and dialogue would be Hemingway's strength, his genius.

Hemingway remained kind to *The Star* in his appreciation of what he had learned at the paper. But *The Star* was not always kind to him. The August 7, 1926, *Star* reviewed Hemingway's newest book. The review, in part, said:

"Young Ernest Hemingway, who left the staff of *The Star* in the early days of the World War [sic], volunteered for the Italian army, and got himself gloriously shot up, has, in spite of it all, not lost his love for shooting. That is proved by his audacious little volume, "Torrents of Spring" ... which is really a machine gun nest peppering ... the literary style of Sherwood Anderson and the Chicago school of fiction."

The review, which bore no initials, referred to Hemingway's first book, *In Our Time*, as mordant, and described *Torrents of Spring* as "dreary," "interminable," and "boring." The reviewer admitted he couldn't finish it.

Oddly, in the years following, hundreds of thousands of others would view the work of Hemingway quite differently.

Rule #1

Use short sentences.

Chapter One

Author as Auteur:
Influences Ephemeral and Enduring

A common project for literary scholars is trying to determine the various influences that shaped the achievement of a prominent writer. What might Nathaniel Hawthorne have read (or experienced) in his formative years that would have prompted him to set so many of his scenes and plots in darkness—at night or in dark rooms? Who in William Faulkner's bookish meanderings suggested that taking liberties with conventional linear narration might make for effective discourse and not chaos? What would we have found on the bookshelves of young Herman Melville, Gertrude Stein, John Steinbeck, and John Updike that would provide clues as to the development of their literary tones and tenors? All writers pass through a phase where, in the search for a literary identity, they absorb material from their reading, their family, and their employment situations that determines what themes they will concern themselves with, and how they will render the words on the page.

While the prose of Ernest Hemingway is an agglomeration of a number of influences that can be divined by a close examination, few writers can be credited with developing a style so distinctive that the term for it contains their name; "Hemingway style" has come to denote a highly direct, highly compressed mode of writing, an antithesis to the embossed descriptive technique employed by most writers prior to Hemingway.

In the world of film, the term *auteur* is used to describe a director whose methods become so closely affiliated with that director that a single clip of their work, based on the idiosyncrasies it contains, is enough to serve as identification. Orson Welles, Fritz Lang, François Truffaut, John Ford, Jane Campion, and Francis Ford Coppola are examples of such auteurs. What Hemingway did was similarly singular: trimming discourse to its nub and producing a new communication experience in a culture where other art forms were already being transformed by Modernism.

Brevity is usually a wise rhetorical strategy. The last thing a reader needs to contend with when reading is an unclear or unfocused text. Hemingway's respect for the double-barreled prescription about brevity in the opening tenet of the *Kansas City Star's* style guide is exemplified by the opening lines of most of his works. Directness and economy are what one has come to expect in the first paragraphs of Hemingway's articles, stories, and novels. The language is simple and, in his fiction, we are drawn almost immediately into the plot. "The marvelous thing is that it's painless ... That's how you know when it starts" is how "The Snows of Kilimanjaro" begins. "It was now lunch time and they were all sitting under the double green fly of the dining tent pretending nothing had happened" throws us right into the situation that "The Short Happy Life of Frances Macomber" is concerned with. The ultimate example of Hemingway's rapid stage setting of a tense situation comes in his story "The Killers," in which his narrator's first words are "The door of Henry's lunch-room opened and two men came in ... They sat down at the counter."

As anyone even slightly familiar with Hemingway is aware, brevity is the dominant characteristic of his work, a characteristic repeated (in one form or another) throughout the *Star*'s rules for its writers. Reading his prose generates the feeling that one is in the presence of expression that has been wound as tightly as possible, lending it the suggestive potential that typically only the best poetry contains. His expression is so charged with potential for elaboration that it is difficult to imagine how any writer could resist letting it all loose in one overwrought and overwritten torrent of words. Writing plainly and concisely was the concrete advice Hemingway was given at the get-go of his career, and he had the good sense to stick to a form that easily could have been dismissed as simplistic, and allowed it to serve as a polestar throughout the course of his career.

The young Hemingway battled uncertainty, and debated which path to choose: a job as a newspaper reporter or enlisting in the military as most of his friends had done. College was open to him, but he was anxious to get started on a career, eager to do something adventurous. He eventually opted for newspaper work, and though he felt guilty not following his buddies abroad, he also knew that he could resign his newspaper position at any time and enlist. Delaying his entrance into the conflict overseas gave Hemingway two advantages: he was able to test his skills as a writer and to think more deeply about what enlisting entailed. In both cases, the benefit was necessary for the youth. He needed to move among professional writers in order to appraise his own abilities, and he needed to be certain that he understood the ramifications of a commitment to military service.

Ultimately, he left the *Star* and headed overseas, knowing that if he was to gather material for the fiction he wanted to write, he had to take on life experiences commensurate with his energetic,

"Hope this doesn't sound over-confident. Am a man without any ambition, except to be champion of the world."

— Hemingway, from a 1949 letter to Charles Scribner

adventurous, and idealistic personality. While he felt they were necessary, Hemingway never could have anticipated how crucial those experiences would be. In serving in the Italian ambulance corps and, later, living in Paris, he placed himself at the center of environments that were ideal for launching a writing career and developing a signature style.

Discourse of the most pragmatic nature does not pay much attention to style. If a writer's purpose is simply to describe or inform, there is no need to be concerned with the nuances that make a piece come alive and spur interest, action, or deep thought. Words set on a page for the most mundane of purposes may be both formally correct and effective, but they will not captivate an audience or serve as a call to action. They are merely functional. Such collections are sometimes described as "plainstyle." Its opposite—whose purpose is to entertain, excite, or enthrall—strives to elevate discourse above the ordinary. In the important reference text *Dictionary of World Literature*, contributor J. C. LaDriere begins his article on the distinction between poetry and prose by noting simply that prose is "ordinary speech" and poetry is speech "which is somehow extraordinary," and then fills the next 12 pages with examples of the "somehow extraordinary." Similarly, prose without freshness and inventiveness is "ordinary"; prose with it is "somehow extraordinary." A world can operate with discourse that is ordinary; in fact, society requires plainstyle language to accomplish most tasks. But to feel significant the world needs to celebrate what language is capable of achieving and showcase what the imagination can do to texturize, amplify, and inspire communication. People are programmed to absorb and/or respond to plainspeak; where we seem to fall short is the ability to utilize, identify, and treasure language's capacity to delight. At his best, Hemingway's prose, plots, and themes are extraordinary in the way he uses his imagination to fire ours.

Dictionary of World Literature contributor E. A. Tenney points out that the word *style* comes from the Latin *stilus*, "an instrument used to write with upon waxed tablets." He who manipulated this instrument "firmly and incisively to make a clear, sharp impression was deemed praiseworthy; his opposite, worthy of blame." Over time, style assumed a metaphorical application, and the idea of "making a sharp impression" was broadened to refer to things other than penmanship—activities like dressing, performing, playing a game, and writing creatively.

In composition, style is everything. It is, according to Plato, what results "when a thought is invested with its essential form." For essayist Walter Pater, style "is the result of the union of beauty and truth, the finer accommodation of speech to that vision within." Style is the most inclusive writing-related term because it is only identifiable—and assessable—after the requisite components have found their place in the execution of a piece. A partial list of those components includes organization, proper grammar, punctuation, tone, voice, point of view, emphasis, and figuration. Without the special processing capabilities of the very talented, however, there is little chance that a given text—chock full of rhetorical devices though it might be—will be memorable, much less achieve *auteur* status. Often enough to justify the acclaim that his life's work generated, Hemingway's processing mechanism functioned optimally and makes us, as acolytes and ambitious learners, want to set out on the examination table the wheels, pulleys, ball bearings, winches, and spindles of that mechanism.

If Hemingway's life is any guide, style is not the product of conscious choice, but of consistently working hard at one's craft.

Hemingway *was* influenced by other writers—by the pedagogical practices of the two high school English teachers whom he truly respected, by the bookish environment of his childhood home, and by instructive documents such as the *Kansas City Star* style guide—but he was not a slave to those influences. In a 1934 list given to a young Arnold Samuelson, who had hitchhiked and then hopped a freight from Minnesota to Key West to ask Hemingway's advice on which writers the young man ought to read to help shape his writing skills, the recommendations included stories by Stephen Crane, Gustave Flaubert's *Madame Bovary*, James Joyce's *The Dubliners*, Stendahl's *The Red and the Black*, W. Somerset Maugham's *Of Human Bondage*, Leo Tolstoy's *Anna Karenina* and *War and Peace*, Thomas Mann's *Buddenbrooks*, George Moore's *Hail and Farewell*, Fyodor Dostoevsky's *Brothers Karamazov*, *The Oxford Book of English Verse*, E. E. Cummings's *The Enormous Room*, Emily Bronte's *Wuthering Heights*, W. H. Hudson's *Far Away and Long Ago*, and Henry James's *The Americans*. Of the authors on that list, none other than Crane could be considered a writer with a tendency toward the compressed expression that is the main feature of Hemingway's prose. In other writings, Hemingway identified Ivan Turgenev, Anton Chekov, and Katherine Ann Porter as writers whom he appreciated.

He read to discover shortcomings in his own writing, and, as he became established as a writer, Hemingway increasingly read to gauge his place in the literary hierarchy. While imagining how he was faring in that competition, he placed himself and his opponents in a "boxing ring." A 1949 letter to his publisher, Charles Scribner, provides some revealing self-assessments: "some matches," Hemingway claims, he would "scrupulously avoid—as with Tolstoy, Shakespeare and 'Mr. Anonymous.'" But he pronounced himself unquestionably victorious in bouts with Turgenev, de Maupassant, Cervantes, and

Henry James ("I would just thumb him once"). Not very subtly, he prefaced his bragging with "Hope this doesn't sound over-confident. Am a man without any ambition, except to be champion of the world." Ford Maddox Ford, Sherwood Anderson, F. Scott Fitzgerald, and one of his early models, Ring Lardner, were also among the group Hemingway considered himself capable of felling.

By the time he was concerned with competition, Hemingway had completely integrated the lessons from the *Star* style guide and other influences, and formed something all his own. While Hemingway spoke so affirmatively about the effect the style guide had on him as a young writer, we can also assume that his lifelong love for literature enabled him to distinguish between those strictures that were practical and those of limited or negligible utility.

The rules—all 110 of them—seem arranged with little concern for logical progression or contiguousness. Only occasionally does a rule have a connection with the rule that precedes or follows it. For example, after the authoritative and universally applicable first rule, the second precept indicates that "The style of local communications is *To the Star*, in italics, out-of-town communications in this form. Salina, Kas. — *To the Star*." The third precept is also a non sequitur: "Never use old slang." Some suggestions must not have been scrutinized for accuracy; the sixth tenet is certain to confuse a reader: "The style of *The Star* is 9:30 o'clock this afternoon." Nevertheless, scrambled as it can be, good advice can be culled from the document.

Several paragraphs in the guide reinforce the opening admonishment to write concisely. Turgidity, which is the antithesis of concision, results from a propensity to use "filler" words and phrases to make a text seem more comprehensive than it is. Too many writers "bloat" their prose in this manner, using sequences of adjectives where the descriptors are synonyms or near synonyms;

"It's none of their business that you have to learn how to write. Let them think you were born that way."

— Advice given to Arnold Samuelson by Hemingway, ca. 1934

by using conjunctive phrases where "and" joins terms that are repetitive rather than complementary (e.g. the road was curvy and winding); by creating whole phrases that use different words to express what has previously been stated. A number of entries in the *Star* style guide are simply illustrations of the introductory thesis about reducing verbiage: "'he said' is better than 'he said in the course of communication,'" and a final reminder about the importance of brevity appears in the last column of the guide: "*Equally as*—the *as* is superfluous."

A factor that ought not be underestimated in examining the key influences on Hemingway is the Modernist movement itself. The subsets of Modernism might be identified, with some overlap, as Futurism, Vorticism, Cubism, Surrealism, and Dada in painting, Expressionism, prevalent in painting but extending into drama, Imagery in poetry, Pure Geometry in architecture, and Minimalism in fiction and several other mediums. Deep dissatisfaction with the way the world defines itself arises every half-century or so, a discontent that promotes the formulation of alternate definitions. Sometimes the sum total of the changes is radical—as was the case in the post-World War I period. Political instability culminating in international warfare and economic destabilization is the most egregious signal of a systemic problem.

Hemingway was still in high school in February 1913 and probably had no awareness of the implications of—or even the occurrence of—the Armory Show on Lexington Avenue in New York City. The show introduced the artistic experiments of Pablo Picasso, Georges Braque, Marcel Duchamp, Henri Matisse, Edvard Munch, Auguste Rodin, and Georges Seurat to a public used to still lifes, landscapes, and portraiture. Nor would Hemingway have sensed that simply by following his instincts he would end up locating a fraternity in which he had already earned membership—amid the artistic community in Paris, the crucible of Modernism.

He was quick to realize a kinship with the architects, sculptors, painters, musicians, composers, psychologists, philosophers, poets, and other writers of fiction who moved through Paris's concentric social circles, groups that disapproved of what the Industrial Age had wrought and sought alternatives to the stale and wrong-minded values of the previous century. In Paris, Hemingway met Gertrude Stein, who proved to be a valuable teacher of the expressional economy. He also met Joyce in Paris and admired the way the Irish writer used elliptical, stream-of-consciousness-drenched passages to carry his narrative experiments. Hemingway found this radically different strategy interesting, but was unwilling to incorporate it into his own approach. He also applauded the lyrical and symbolically complex prose his friend F. Scott Fitzgerald used in *The Great Gatsby*, though Hemingway eventually came to believe that Fitzgerald squandered his talent and betrayed the Modernist movement by valuing commercial success more than the creation of new literary forms.

Difficult as they are to date with accuracy, three stories that were written either when Hemingway returned from Italy or during his seven months with the *Kansas City Star* appeared in a 1923 collection titled *Three Stories and Ten Poems*. These stories provide a clear glimpse of Hemingway working his way through dilemmas of style and theme, determining which of the skills he'd used as a reporter might be transferable to fiction, and how to utilize his vivid imagination now that there were no journalistic limitations to contend with. These stories also show his determination that the straightforward prose he'd been trained to use at the *Star* was a solid foundation for the experiences that propelled his narratives.

"My Old Man," which appeared in that collection, is an outstanding piece of writing, whatever the age of its author. Told from the point of view of Joe, a boy aged somewhere from 10 to 12, the story features the youth's reflections on his father after the older man, who is a jockey, dies in a riding accident. The boy is intelligent and respectful toward his father, even as his exploration dredges up issues with his father's character. In a story that might have tempted a less-skilled writer to add a thick layer of sentimentality to the narrative's final sections, Hemingway stays the course, even when detailing the grief of a boy who finds himself suddenly and absolutely alone. Each expression from the boy is perfectly in character, consonant with the figure we are given at the story's beginning. While he is deeply dismayed, the strengths instilled by his Elmer Gantry–like father allow him to carry on. And the ending, though sad, is without bathos.

Perhaps a word on the subject of concision is in order. The *Star's* prescriptions about shortening sentences and paragraphs are placed at the top of the first column to alert new reporters that padded expression and circumlocution were no longer acceptable in news stories. The rule is more metonymic than literal: direct writing does consist of tight sentences and paragraphs, but it is not the only way direct speech can be achieved. Larger units of description do not necessarily constitute excess; the challenge for the writer comes in determining where the line separating essential from superfluous discourse lies. Any writer's strategy should include an implicit understanding that gratuitous material has no place in dialogue, exposition, or description. Elaboration, however, is not evil when it unveils the essential. That the "Hemingway style" has been identified almost exclusively as consisting of starkly simple sentences interwoven with equally unadorned compound sentences is only part of the reality. Hemingway's narrative and nonfiction pieces often do begin with noticeably brief sentences, and they continue in that vein elsewhere. But Hemingway was certainly aware that a surfeit of short sentences can undermine the positive effect direct prose can have. The "necessary but sufficient" maxim applies here. The lesson of compact expression is not vitiated if the particulars of a description are essential and rendered economically. Being brief and maintaining *a spirit of brevity* is what the *Star's* lead precepts are more accurately about.

In the first medium-length paragraphs of "My Old Man," it is difficult to see what descriptive information could be excised. The speaker throughout the piece is young Joe and his subject is always his father: traveling with his father, watching his father ride racehorses, commenting on his father's efforts to stay in shape, and listening to his father's sound advice on a variety of topics. Joe has a lot to fill in regarding his relationship with his father before getting to his father's fatal ride, but his account never seems excessive.

Stein always pushed for even further trimming in the manuscripts Hemingway handed her, but in "My Old Man," even she would struggle to find something that could be cut without sacrificing essential information about the story's two characters, the story's setting, and, since the story is a *bildungsroman* (a "growing-up" story), a young person's psychological constitution. It is clear that the structural integrity of the story would be critically compromised absent the staging that Hemingway provides. Striving for verisimilitude does not mean hacking away at a story's details simply to conform to the minimalist inclinations of Modernism. The longer paragraphs in Hemingway's fiction are as trim as they can be without sacrificing functionality. Dialogue ought to be free from senseless digression, but even digressions can be functional when they enhance credibility. "This is how people really speak" is the only sensible response.

"Write the best story that you can and write it as straight as you can."

— From A Moveable Feast

These early paragraphs are—in line with the Modernist credo—both *necessary* and *sufficient.*

The dialogue in this story, however, may be described as frugal and functional. The primary way we receive information is through Joe's first-person accounts: directly about the father based on the assessments of the son, and inferentially about the son, whose personality can be pieced together by reading between the lines of his address. In the first 12 paragraphs only 10 phrases or sentences—less than 100 words—are in dialogue form. And the pattern continues until the story's end, with the exception of two key places, the appearance of which make it clear that Hemingway has chosen to judiciously wield the power that succinct dialogue (or, in the second case, quoted speech) can possess. In the first instance, brief exchanges between father and son make it plain that the race between Kzar and Kircubbin was fixed, and that the father, who is seen pocketing a large wad of bills, was in on it. The father says, "George Gardner's a swell jockey, all right ... It sure took a great jock to keep that Kzar from winning." It is the first time the son is forced to wonder whether his father is the highly principled individual he had always believed. The second instance comes in the story's final lines, when Hemingway uses comments Joe overhears to reveal vital information. Joe is standing close enough to a track regular to hear the man say about his father, "Well, Butler got his all right." The man's companion responds, "I don't give a good goddam if he did, the crook. He had it coming to him on the stuff he's pulled." Gardner, standing close to Joe, tries to soften the blow with "Don't you listen to what those bums said, Joe. Your old man was one swell guy." But the seed is planted, and, in an early example of what became a patented way for Hemingway to close a story, Joe frames a thought that will shape the rest of his life: "But I don't know. Seems like when they get started they don't leave a guy nothing."

My Old Man

I guess looking at it now my old man was cut out for a fat guy, one of those regular little roly fat guys you see around, but he sure never got that way, except a little toward the last, and then it wasn't his fault, he was riding over the jumps only and he could afford to carry plenty of weight then. I remember the way he'd pull on a rubber shirt over a couple of jerseys and a big sweat shirt over that, and get me to run with him in the forenoon in the hot sun. He'd have, maybe, taken a trial trip with one of Razzo's skins early in the morning after just getting in from Torino at four o'clock in the morning and beating it out to the stables in a cab and then with the dew all over everything and the sun just starting to get going, I'd help him pull off his boots and he'd get into a pair of sneakers and all these sweaters and we'd start out.

"Come on, kid," he'd say, stepping up and down on his toes in front of the jock's dressing room, "let's get moving."

Then we'd start off jogging around the infield once maybe with him ahead running nice and then turn out the gate and along one of those roads with all the trees along both sides of them that run out from San Siro. I'd go ahead of him when we hit the road and I could run pretty stout and I'd look around and he'd be jogging easy just behind me and after a little while I'd look around again and he'd begun to sweat. Sweating heavy and he'd just he clogging it along with his eyes on my back, but when he'd catch me looking at him he'd grin and say, "Sweating plenty?" When my old man grinned nobody could help but grin too. We'd keep right on running out toward the mountains and then my old man would yell "Hey Joe!" and I'd look back and he'd be sitting under a tree with a towel he'd had around his waist wrapped around his neck.

I'd come back and sit down beside him and he'd pull a rope out of his pocket and start skipping rope out in the sun with the sweat pouring off his face and him skipping rope out in the white dust with the rope going cloppetty cloppetty clop clop clop and the sun hotter and him working harder up and down a patch of the road. Say it was a treat to see my old man skip rope too. He could whirr it fast or lop it slow and fancy. Say you ought to have seen wops look at us sometimes when they'd come by going into town walking along with big white steers hauling the cart. They sure looked as though they thought the old man was nuts. He'd start the rope whirring till they'd stop dead still and watch him, then give the steers a cluck and a poke with the goad and get going again.

When I'd sit watching him working out in the hot sun I sure felt fond of him. He sure was fun and he done his work so hard and he'd finish up with a regular whirring that'd drive the sweat out on his face like water and then sling the rope at the tree and come over and sit down with me and lean back against the tree with the towel and a sweater wrapped around his neck.

"Sure is hell keeping it down, Joe," he'd say and lean back and shut his eyes and breath long and deep, "it ain't like when you're a kid". Then he'd get up before he started to cool and we'd jog along back to the stables. That's the way it was keeping down to weight. He was worried all the time. Most jocks can just about ride off all they want to. A jock loses about a kilo every time he rides, but my old man was sort of dried out and he couldn't keep down his kilos without all that running.

I remember once at San Siro, Regoli, a little wop that was riding for Buzoni came out across the paddock going to the bar for something cool and flicking his bouts with his whip, after he'd just weighed in and my old man had just weighed in too and came out with the saddle under his arm looking red faced and tired and too big for his silks and he stood there looking at young Regoli standing up to the outdoors bar cool and kid looking and I says, "What's the matter, Dad?" cause I thought maybe Regoli had bumped him or something and he just looked at Regoli and said, "Oh to hell with it," and went on to the dressing room.

Well it would have been all right maybe if we'd stayed in Milan and ridden at Milan and Torino cause if there ever were any easy courses its those two. "Pianola, Joe". My old man said when he dismounted in the winning stall after what the wops thought was a hell of a steeplechase. I asked him once, "This course rides its-self. It's the pace you're going at that makes riding the jumps dangerous, Joe. We aint going any pace here, and they aint any really bad jumps either. But it's the pace always—not the jumps that makes the trouble".

San Siro was the swellest course I'd ever seen but the old man said it was a dog's life. Going back and forth between Mirafiore and San Siro and riding just about every day in the week with a train ride every other night.

I was nuts about the horses too. There's something about it when they come out and go up the track to the post. Sort of dancy and tight looking with the jock keeping a tight hold on them and maybe easing off a little and letting them run a little going up. Then once they were at the barrier it got me worse than anything. Especially at San Siro with that big green infield and the mountains way off and the fat wop starter with his big whip and the jocks fiddling them around and then the barrier snapping up and that bell going off and them all getting off in a bunch and then commencing to string out. You know the way a bunch of skins gets off. If you're up in the stand with a pair of glasses all you see is them plunging off and then that bell goes off and it seems like it rings for a thousand years and then they come sweeping round the turn. There wasn't ever anything like it for me.

But my old man said one day in the dressing room when he was getting into his street clothes, "None of these things are horses, Joe. They'd kill that bunch of skates for their hides and hoofs up at Paris". That was the day he'd won the Premio Commercio with Lantorna shooting her out of the field the last hundred meters like pulling a cork out of a bottle.

It was right after the Premio Commercio that we pulled out and left Italy. My old man and Holbrook and a fat wop in a straw hat that kept wiping his face with a handkerchief were having an argument at a table in the Galleria. They were all talking French and the two of them were after my old man about something. Finally he didn't say anything any more but just sat there and looked at Holbrook and the two of them kept after him, first one talking and then the other, and the fat wop always butting in on Holbrook.

"You go out and buy me a *Sportsman*, will you, Joe?" my old man said and handed me a couple of soldi without looking away from Holbrook.

So I went out of the Galleria and walked over to in front of the Scala and bought a paper and came back and stood a little way away because I didn't want to butt in and my old man was sitting back in his chair looking down at his coffee and fooling with a spoon and Holbrook and the big wop were standing and the big wop was wiping his face and shaking his head. And I came up and my old man acted just as though the two of them weren't standing there and said, "Want an ice, Joe?" Holbrook looked down at my old man and said slow and careful, "You son of a bitch" and he and the fat wop went out through the tables.

My old man sat there and sort of smiled at me but his face was white and he looked sick as hell and I was scared and felt sick inside because I knew something had happened and I didn't see how anybody could call my old man a son of a bitch and get away with it. My old man opened up the *Sportsman* and studied the handicaps for a while and then he said, "You got to take a lot of things in this world, Joe". And three days later we left Milan for good on the Turin train for Paris after an auction sale out in front of Turner's stables of everything we couldn't get into a trunk and a suit case.

We got into Paris early in the morning in a long dirty station the old man told me was the Gare de Lyon. Paris was an awful big town after Milan. Seems like in Milan everybody is going somewhere and all the trams run somewhere and there ain't any sort of a mixup, but Paris is all balled up and they never do straighten it out. I got to like it though, part of it anyway, and say it's got the best race courses in the world. Seems as though that were the thing that keeps it all going and about the only thing you can figure on is that every day the buses will be going out to whatever track they're running at going right out through everything to the track. I never really got to know Paris well because I just came in about once or twice a week with the old man from Maisons and he always sat at the Cafe de la Paix on the Opera side with the rest of the gang from Maisons and I guess that's one of the busiest parts of the town. But say it is funny that a big town like Paris wouldn't have a Galleria isn't it?

Well, we went out to live at Maisons-Lafitte, where just about everybody lives except the gang at Chantilly, with a Mrs. Meyers that runs a boarding house. Maisons is about the swellest place to live I've ever seen in all my life. The town ain't so much, but there's a lake and a swell forest that we used to go off humming in all day, a couple of us kids, and my old man made me a sling shot and we got a lot of things with it but the best one was a magpie. Young Dick Atkinson shot a rabbit with it one day and we put it under a tree and were all sitting around and Dick had some cigarettes and all of a sudden the rabbit jumped up and beat it into the brush and we chased it but we couldn't find it. Gee we had fun at Maisons. Mrs. Meyers used to give me lunch in the morning and I'd be gone all day. I learned to talk French quick. It's an easy language.

As soon as we got to Maisons my old man wrote to Milan for his license and he was pretty worried till it came. He used to sit around the Cafe de Paris in Maisons with the gang there, there were lots of guys he'd known when he rode up at Paris, before the war, lived at Maisons, and there's a lot of time to sit around because the work around a racing stable, for the jocks that is, is all cleaned up by nine o'clock in the morning. They take the first batch of skins out to gallop them at 5:30 in the morning and they work the second lot at 8 o'clock. That means getting up early all right and going to bed early too. If a jock's riding for somebody too he can't go boozing around because the trainer always has an eye on him if he's a kid and if he ain't a kid he's always got an eye on himself. So mostly if a jock ain't working he sits around the Cafe de Paris with the gang and they can all sit around about two or three hours in front of some drink like a vermouth and seltz and they talk and tell stories and shoot pool and it's sort of like a club or the Galleria in Milan. Only it ain't really like the Galleria because there everybody is going by all the time and there's everybody around at the tables.

Well my old man got his license all right. They sent it through to him without a word and he rode a couple of times. Amiens, up country and that sort of thing, but he didn't seem to get any engagement. Everybody liked him and whenever I'd come in to the Café in the forenoon I'd find somebody drinking with him because my old man wasn't tight like most of these jockeys that have got the first dollar they made riding at the World's Fair in St. Louis in Nineteen ought four. That's what my old man would say when he'd kid George Burns. But it seemed like everybody steered clear of giving my old man any mounts.

We went out to wherever they were running every day with the car from Maisons and that was the most fun of all. I was glad when the horses came back from Deauville and the summer. Even though it meant no more humming in the woods, cause then we'd ride to Enghien or Tremblay or St. Cloud and watch them from the trainers' and jockeys' stand. I sure learned about racing from going out with that gang and the fun of it was going every day.

I remember once out at St. Cloud. It was a big two hundred thousand franc race with seven entries and Kzar a big favourite. I went around to the paddock to see the horses with my old man and you never saw such horses. This Kzar is a great big yellow horse that looks like just nothing but run. I never saw such a horse. He was being led around the paddock with his head down and when he went by me I felt all hollow inside he was so beautiful. There never was such a wonderful, lean, running built horse. And he went around the paddock putting his feet just so and quiet and careful and moving easy like he knew just what he had to do and not jerking and standing up on his legs and getting wild eyed like you see these selling platers with a shot of dope in them. The crowd was so thick I couldn't see him again except just his legs going by and some yellow and my old man started out through the crowd and I followed him over to the jock's dressing room back in the trees and there was a big crowd around there too but the man at the door in a derby nodded to my old man and we got in and everybody was sitting around and getting dressed and pulling shirts over their heads and pulling boots on and it all smelled hot and sweaty and linimenty and outside was the crowd looking in.

The old man went over and sat down beside George Gardner that was getting into his pants and said, "What's the dope, George?" just in an ordinary tone of voice cause there ain't any use him feeling around because George either can tell him or he can't tell him.

"He won't win," George says very low, leaning over and buttoning the bottoms of his pants.

"Who will," my old man says leaning over close so nobody can hear.

"Kircubbin," George says, "And if he does, save me a couple of tickets."

My old man says something in a regular voice to George and George says, "Don't ever bet on anything I tell you," kidding like and we beat it out and through all the crowd that was looking in over to the 100 franc mutuel machine. But I knew something big was up because George is Kzar's jockey. On the way he gets one of the yellow odds sheets with the starting prices on and Kzar is only paying 5 for 10, Cefisidote is next at 3 to 1 and fifth down the list this Kircubbin at 8 to 1. My old man bets five thousand on Kircubbin to win and puts on a thousand to place and we went around back of the grandstand to go up the stairs and get a place to watch the race.

We were jammed in tight and first a man in a long coat with a gray tall hat and a whip folded up in his hand came out and then one after another the horses, with the jocks up and a stable boy holding the bridle on each side and walking along, followed the old guy.

That big yellow horse Kzar came first. He didn't look so big when you first looked at him until you saw the length of his legs and the whole way he's built and the way he moves. Gosh, I never saw such a horse. George Gardner was riding him and they moved along slow, back of the old guy in the gray tall hat that walked along like he was the ring master in a circus. Back of Kzar, moving along smooth and yellow in the sun, was a good-looking black with a nice head with Tommy Archibald riding him and after the black was a string of five more horses all moving along slow in a procession past the grandstand and the pesage. My old man said the black was Kircubbin and I took a good look at him and he was a nice looking horse all right but nothing like Kzar.

Everybody cheered Kzar when he went by and he sure was one swell looking horse. The procession of them went around on the other side past the pelouse and then back up to the near end of the course and the circus master had the stable boys turn them loose one after another so they could gallop by the stands on their way up to the post and let everybody have a good look at them. They weren't at the post hardly any time at all when the gong started and you could see them way off across the infield all in a bunch starting on the first swing like a lot of little toy horses. I was watching them through the glasses and Kzar was running well back with one of the bays making the pace. They swept down and around and came pounding past and Kzar was way back when they passed us and this Kircubbin horse in front and going smooth. Gee it's awful when they go by you and then you have to watch them go farther away and get smaller and smaller and then all bunched up on the turns and then come around towards into the stretch and you feel like swearing and goddaming worse and worse. Finally they made the last turn and came into the straightaway with this Kircubbin horse way out in front. Everybody was looking funny and saying "Kzar" in sort of a sick way and them pounding nearer down the stretch, and then something came out of the pack right into my glasses like a horse-headed yellow streak and everybody began to yell "Kzar" as though they were crazy. Kzar came on faster than I'd ever seen anything in my life and pulled up on Kircubbin that was going fast as any black horse could go with the jock flogging hell out of him with the gad and they were right dead neck and neck for a second but Kzar seemed going about twice as fast with those great jumps and that head out—but it was while they were neck and neck that they passed the winning post and when the numbers went up in the slots the first one was 2 and that meant Kircubbin had won.

I felt all trembly and funny inside, and then we were all jammed in with the people going downstairs to stand in front of the board where they'd post what Kircubbin paid. Honest, watching the race I'd forgot how much my old man had bet on Kircubbin. I'd wanted Kzar to win so damned bad. But now it was all over it was swell to know we had the winner.

"Wasn't it a swell race, Dad?" I said to him.

He looked at me sort of funny with his derby on the back of his head. "George Gardner's a swell jockey all right," he said. "It sure took a great jock to keep that Kzar horse from winning."

Of course I knew it was funny all the time. But my old man saying that right out like that sure took the kick all out of it for me and I didn't get the real kick back again ever, even when they posted the numbers up on the board and the bell rang to pay off and we saw that Kircubbin paid 67.50 for 10. All around people were saying, "Poor Kzar. Poor Kzar!" And I thought, I wish I were a jockey and could have rode him instead of that son of a bitch. And that was funny, thinking of George Gardner as a son of a bitch because I'd always liked him, and besides he'd given us the winner, but I guess that's what he is all right.

My old man had a big lot of money after that race and he took to coming into Paris oftener. If they raced at Tremblay he'd have them drop him in town on their way back to Maisons and he and I'd sit out in front of the Café de la Paix and watch the people go by. It's funny sitting there. There's streams of people going by and all sorts of guys come up and want to sell you things and I loved to sit there with my old man. That was when we'd have the most fun. Guys would come by selling funny rabbits that jumped if you squeezed a bulb and they'd come up to us and my old man would kid with them. He could talk French just like English and all those kind of guys knew him cause you can always tell a jockey and then we always sat at the same table and they got used to seeing us there. There were guys selling matrimonial papers and girls selling rubber eggs that when you squeezed them a rooster came out of them and one old wormy looking guy that went by with post cards of Paris showing them to everybody, and of course nobody ever bought any and then he would come back and show the underside of the pack and they would all be smutty post cards and lots of people would dig down and buy them.

Gee I remember the funny people that used to go by. Girls around supper time looking for somebody to take them out to eat and they'd speak to my old man and he'd make some joke at them in French and they'd pat me on the head and go on. Once there was an American woman sitting with her kid daughter at the next table to us and they were both eating ices and I kept looking at the girl and she was awfully good looking and I smiled at her and she smiled at me but that was all that ever came of it because I looked for her mother and her every day and I made up ways that I was going to speak to her and I wondered if I get to know her if her mother would let me take her out to Auteuil or Tremblay but I never saw either of them again. Anyway I guess it wouldn't have been any good anyway because looking back on it I remember the way I thought out would be best to speak to her was to say, "Pardon me, but perhaps I can give you a winner at Enghien today?" and after all maybe she would have thought I was a tout instead of really trying to give her a winner.

We'd sit at the Café de la Paix, my old man and me, and we had a big drag with the waiter because my old man drank whisky and it cost five francs and that meant a good tip when the saucers were counted up. My old man was drinking more than I'd ever seen him, but he wasn't riding at all now and besides he said that whiskey kept his weight down. But I noticed he was putting it on all right just the same. He'd busted away from his old gang out at Maisons and seemed to like just sitting around on the boulevard with me. But he was dropping money every day at the track. He'd feel sort of doleful after the last race, if he'd lost on the day, until we'd get to our table and he'd have his first whiskey and then he'd be fine.

He'd be reading the *Paris-Sport* and he'd look over at me and say, "Where's your girl, Joe?" to kid me on account I had told him about the girl that day at the next table. And I'd get red but I liked being kidded about her. It gave me a good feeling. "Keep your eye peeled for her, Joe," he'd say. "She'll be back."

He'd ask me questions about things and some of the things I'd say he'd laugh. And then he'd get started talking about things. About riding down in Egypt, or at St. Moritz on the ice before my mother died, and about during the war when they had regular races down in the south of France without any purses, or betting or crowd or anything just to keep the breed up. Regular races with the jocks riding hell out of the horses. Gee, I could listen to my old man talk by the hour, especially when he'd had a couple or so of drinks. He'd tell me about when he was a boy in Kentucky and going coon hunting and the old days in the states before everything went on the bum there. And he'd say, "Joe, when we've get a decent stake, you're going back there to the States and go to school."

"What've I get to go back there to go to school for when everything's on the bum there?" I'd ask him.

"That's different," he'd say and get the waiter over and pay the pile of saucers and we'd get a taxi to the Gare St. Lazare and get on the train out to Maisons.

One day at Auteuil after a selling steeplechase my old man bought in the winner for 30,000 francs. He had to bid a little to get him but the stable let the horse go finally and my old man had his permit and his colors in a week. Gee I felt proud when my old man was an owner. He fixed it up for stable space with Charles Drake and cut out coming in to Paris and started his running and sweating out again and him and I were the whole stable gang. Our horse's name was Gillford, he was Irish bred and a nice sweet jumper. My old man figured that training him and riding him himself he was a good investment. I was proud of everything and I thought Gillford was as good a horse as Kzar. He was a good solid jumper, a bay, with plenty of speed on the flat if you asked him for it and he was a nice looking horse too.

Gee I was fond of him. The first time he started with my old man up he finished third in a 2,500 meter hurdle race and when my old man got off him, all sweating and happy in the place stall and went in to weigh I felt as proud of him as though it was the first race he'd ever placed in. You see when a guy ain't been riding for a long time you can't make yourself really believe that he has ever rode. The whole thing was different now cause down in Milan even big races never seemed to make any difference to my old man, if he won he wasn't ever excited or anything, and now it was so I couldn't hardly sleep the night before a race and I knew my old man was excited too even if he didn't show it. Riding for yourself makes an awful difference.

Second time Gillford and my old man started was a rainy Sunday at Auteuil in the Prix du Marat, a 4,500 meter steeplechase. As soon as he'd gone out I beat it up in the stand with the new glasses my old man had bought for me to watch them. They started way over at the far end of the course and there was some trouble at the barrier. Something with goggle blinders on was making a great fuss and roaring around and busted the barrier once but I could see my old man in our black jacket with a white cross and a black cap sitting up on Gillford and patting him with his hand. Then they were off in a jump and out of sight behind the trees and the gong going for dear life and the pari mutuel wickets rattling down. Gosh I was so excited I was afraid to look at them but I fixed the glasses on the place where they would come out back of the trees and then out they came with the old black jacket going third and they all sailing over the jump like birds. Then they went out of sight again and then they came pounding out and down the hill and all going nice and sweet and easy and taking the fence smooth in a bunch and moving away from us all solid. Looked as though you could walk across on their backs they were all so hunched and going so smooth. Then they bellied over the big double Bullfinch and something came down. I couldn't see who it was but in a minute the horse was up and galloping free and the field, all bunched still, sweeping around the long left turn into the straightaway. They jumped the stone wall and came jammed down the stretch toward the big water jump right in front of the stands. I saw them coming and hollered at my old man as he went by and he was leading by about a length and riding way out over and light as a monkey and they were racing for the water jump. They took off over the big hedge of the water jump in a pack and then there was a crash and two horses pulled sideways out off it and kept on going and three others were piled up. I couldn't see my old man anywhere. One horse kneed himself up and the jock had hold of the bridle and mounted and went slamming on after the place money. The other horse was up and away by himself, jerking his head and galloping with the bridle rein hanging and the jock staggered over to one side of the track against the fence. Then Gillford rolled over to one side off my old man and got up and started to run on three legs with his off hoof dangling and there was my old man lying there on the grass flat out with his face up and blood all over the side of his head. I ran down the stand and bumped into a jam of people and got to the rail and a cop grabbed me and held me and two big stretcher bearers were going out after my old man and around on the other side of the course I saw three horses, strung way out, coming out of the trees and taking the jump.

My old man was dead when they brought him in and while a doctor was listening to his heart with a thing plugged in his ears I heard a shot up the track that meant they'd killed Gillford. I lay down beside my old man when they carried the stretcher into the hospital room and hung onto the stretcher and cried and cried and he looked so white and gone and so awfully dead and I couldn't help feeling that if my old man was dead maybe they didn't need to have shot Gillford. His hoof might have got well. I don't know. I loved my old man so much.

Then a couple of guys came in and one of them patted me on the back and then went over and looked at my old man and then pulled a sheet off the cot and spread it over him; and the other was telephoning in French for them to send the ambulance to take him out to Maisons. And I couldn't stop crying, crying and choking, sort of, and George Gardner came in and sat down beside me on the floor and put his arm around me and says, "Come on, Joe old boy. Get up and we'll go out and wait for the ambulance."

George and I went out to the gate and I was trying to stop bawling and George wiped off my face with his handkerchief and we were standing back a little ways while the crowd was going out of the gate and a couple of guys stopped near us while we were waiting for the crowd to get through the gate and one of them was counting a bunch of mutuel tickets and he said, "Well, Butler got his all right."

The other guy said, "I don't give a good goddam if he did, the crook. He had it coming to him on the stuff he's pulled."

"I'll say he had," said the other guy and tore the bunch of tickets in two.

And George Gardner looked at me to see if I'd heard and I had all right and he said, "Don't you listen to what those bums said, Joe. Your old man was one swell guy."

But I don't know. Seems like when they get started they don't leave a guy nothing.

Rule #2

Avoid the use of adjectives, especially such extravagant ones as splendid, gorgeous, grand, magnificent, etc.

Chapter Two

Discourse about Discourse: Striking the Right Note (Without Getting Injured)

American literature had hardly made a mark on the world's literary scene when Hemingway was a student. Melville was dead and his masterwork, *Moby-Dick*, remained an enigma that was largely ignored by critics and readers. Emerson enjoyed a limited following of scholars and theologians. The American "Fireside Poets"—John Greenleaf Whittier, Henry Wadsworth Longfellow, James Russell Lowell, and William Cullen Bryant—had some currency, but only because their poetry imitated the genre's English deans: Samuel Taylor Coleridge, John Keats, Lord Byron, Percy Bysshe Shelley, John Milton, Alexander Pope, and Robert Browning. The world had yet to discover Walt Whitman, and no one had heard of Emily Dickinson.

Hemingway's English class at Oak Park High School was precisely that, a place where the only books available were those authored by British writers. The class even met in the "Oxford Room," a space specifically decorated with tall, stained-glass windows, polished wainscoting, high-backed oak chairs, and a large fireplace. Over time, Hemingway would acknowledge the important influence many of the works he encountered during this time had on him. But it was the hard-to-come-by books authored by Americans that excited him about the possibility of becoming a writer. Considered too banal to be granted shelf space, the fiction of Frank Norris, Theodore Dreiser, and Upton Sinclair was unavailable to Hemingway, who had to wait until 1916 before he was even able to locate a contraband copy of Stephen Crane's *The Red Badge of Courage*.

Nevertheless, in this rather myopic literary environment, Hemingway came to appreciate the energetic discourse of Rudyard Kipling and the rough-and-tumble prose of Ring Lardner. Hemingway biographer Kenneth Lynn describes Ernest's family as "Anglophile" and reports that the bookshelves in their Oak Park home were stacked with editions of William Shakespeare, Sir Walter Scott, Charles Dickens, William Makepeace Thackeray, and Robert Louis Stevenson. The young Hemingway had to scour the neighborhood for the non-British fiction he felt would be more useful to his writerly aspirations. The imitations of Jack London's mannerisms and the adventure-based prose of Theodore Roosevelt and Owen Wister that appear in Hemingway's early story drafts indicate that he was successful in making some headway into the early American literary tradition. The young Hemingway was also struck by what Mark Twain had done to invest the hero-narrator of *The Adventures of Huckleberry Finn* with a completely believable Mississippi River patois. Lynn believes that he had also read Edgar Rice Burroughs's *Tarzan of the Apes* adventure series. Somewhere during this period of absorption and emulation, Hemingway developed enough confidence to share his plans to become a writer with his parents—with the first phase of that plan involving work as a war correspondent.

Several items of instruction in the *Kansas City Star's* style guide pertain to the types of discourse germane to newspaper writing. Innovative as Twain's use of provincial speech was, there was no place in the pages of the *Star* for such linguistic realism—with the exception of phrases enclosed within quotation marks—nor was there justification for a reporter submitting copy that in any way imitated London's muscular prose. Illustrations of the direct speech required of all *Star* reporters are sprinkled throughout the style guide. "The police tried to find her husband ... not locate her husband" is followed by the explanation that *locate*, as a transitive verb, means to establish. "The thief seized her purse, not grabbed or snatched." Whatever is wrong with grabbed or snatched is not stipulated. "Smith asserted he had been arrested falsely, not claimed he had been arrested." No qualifying explanation here, either. It seems that new reporters were expected to memorize the paper's standards of correct usage and not question the logic behind them.

On the broader matter of proper and consistent usage, reporters are reminded that a newspaper's role is to gather and disseminate news in a way that is not confusing to its readership. The intent of the story—to outline current events, paraphrase an argument, relate an account, or explain a process—determines the diction, tone, and length, as well as which factual particulars needed coverage. Louis H. Sullivan, Modernist architect and philosophical force behind the 1893 Chicago Exposition, could have been addressing the central thesis of the *Star* guide when he uttered the famous phrase, "Let the form be determined by the function." According to the guide, the core details of the story, not the impressions of the writer toward those details, take precedence.

When the *Star* style sheet rails against the use of "old slang" ("Never use old slang. Such words as stunt, cut out, got his goat, come across, sit up and take notice, put one over, have no place after their use becomes common") yet sanctions other uses of slang ("Slang to be enjoyable must be fresh"), what the document makes clear is that, at any level of language usage, consistency, concision, and currency are the guideposts.

Most recent treatises on linguistics identify several tiers of written and spoken standard English, from the highest—texts that are more or less in complete conformity with the generally accepted rules and regulations—down to the lowest: verbal communication that is either substandard and only marginally acceptable ("correct enough") or not acceptable because the errors have terminally compromised the meaning. Journalism generally demands mid-level compliance, whether the assignment is to cover election results in a small town or produce an editorial. Dispassion in the attitude of the reporter is essential as well, as is an avoidance of exaggeration in the account. "Avoid the use of extravagant adjectives," warns the style guide, an admonishment guided by the belief that the target audience is not going to have the patience to decipher the intricacies of elevated discourse. The *Star's* proscription against old slang is also a warning to reporters to use a voice that is familiar to a reader and remains consistent all the way through.

Hemingway's stint at the *Kansas City Star* gave him little latitude for investigating language's creative possibilities. Where straightforward prose is required—reports, operating instructions, directions, summaries, and nondramatic narratives—the language must be, above all, clear and correct. But what Hemingway lacked in leeway and creative freedom, he gained in establishing a solid prose foundation. As the best pictorial artists tend to perfect the fundamentals before advancing to more expressive creations, his time at the paper provided Hemingway with an opportunity to learn the lessons of straightforward writing. It was a pragmatic base that would eventually support the experimental kind of fiction he knew

"Prose is architecture, not interior decoration, and the Baroque is over."

— From Death in the Afternoon

he was capable of generating, even, or perhaps especially, when the subject matter was as sensitive as abortion, death, and rape.

"Hills Like White Elephants" (1927) provides a perfect example of Hemingway's mastery of managing discourse. The incident is related by a speaker who is not part of the drama. His narratorial responsibilities are minimal: place two characters in a setting, and then record the conversation that occurs between them. Hemingway, of course, is the "puppet master" determining the particulars of the plot and how to render the drama of those particulars most effectively. Hemingway's most striking rhetorical device is a "dialogic stacking" where the couple's dilemma is revealed via an unusually extended sequence of conversational exchanges. The typical demarcations of who is speaking (i.e. dialogue tags: "he/she said") are virtually absent in these exchanges. Though our ability to follow who is saying what is severely taxed by the device, it nevertheless works, to the degree that it became a signature device in Hemingway's fiction. In these circumstances, readers are obliged to pay close attention to speaker-identities as a dialogue unfolds. Without diminishing Flaubert's theory that "character is plot," Hemingway had added a corollary that "dialogue could also be plot."

Why place such a heavy burden on the dialogue? It is an effective way, without the distraction of description, of centering the dilemma—in "Hills Like White Elephants, an abortion and the future of the couple's relationship—around those it most concerns. Where the man and woman are and what they look like are of little significance in this mode. By privileging their conversation as the key plot device, remaining neutral as a narrator, offering little more than brief expositions and clinical descriptions, and minimizing the use of dialogue tags, Hemingway allows the characters a unique way to propel a story line. It also allows for an immediate connection between the reader and the characters. Assessments about which of the two principals has the moral high ground can be made (or seem to be made) more or less without the prejudicial shadings a narrator/intermediary might interject. What, then, can we infer from what we "overhear" about whom we should respect and whom not? The woman has our sympathy; the man does not. The language the dialogue consists of is casual, highly personal, and naturally nuanced. The narrator—detached from the "action" of the story—is, more or less, a reporter.

What registers prominently with "Indian Camp," an early story featuring Nick Adams, Hemingway's thinly-disguised alter ego, is the control he exercises. With only a few adjustments to how the story is presented (notably a damping down of the drama of the throat-cutting scene at the end), the account of a boy's very purposeful trip into the backwoods with his physician father might even have been acceptable to the editors of the *Star* as a feature about a boy's life-changing experience. Published in 1924 in Ford Maddox Ford's *Transatlantic Review*, the starkly straightforward discourse found in "Indian Camp" indicates that Hemingway's newspaper training in Kansas City was still a major stylistic influence. There is heavy drama in the story—and a serious theme related to how fathers influence their sons—but drama and theme are carried off without overwriting or melodrama. It is simply a good story told well, and a solid template for all Hemingway's fiction that would follow.

Drama—whatever it might turn out to be—is inherent in the story's second sentence: "The two Indians stood waiting." Nick, his father, his uncle, and the two Native Americans make their way in the early morning hours via a camp boat across a lake to a shanty where a Native American woman had been trying "for two days" to have her baby. The woman's husband, apparently exhausted, sleeps in an

"A writer who omits things because he does not know them only makes hollow places in his writing."

— From Death in the Afternoon

upper bunk against the wall. Young Nick holds a basin for his father as he takes charge over a rough and grossly unsanitary birthing, all of which Nick takes in. In prose both graphic and appropriate for the occasion, the narrator captures, most importantly, and all at once, Nick's introduction to life and death as the baby is born and the revelation that the baby's father bled to death after slashing his throat in his bunk.

Hemingway's understated closing scene finds Nick and his father rowing back across the lake. The son's questions about what he has just witnessed are poignant. Hemingway's backdrop to the father's responses indicates a writer who already knows much about the dangers of sentimentalized discourse. As the son carefully phrases his questions—"Why did he kill himself, Daddy?"; "Do many men kill themselves, Daddy?"; " Is dying hard, Daddy?"—Nick sits in the stern of the rowboat while his father rows and deliberates how to respond to his son's calm questions. The optimistic—but not sentimentalized—tableau Hemingway leaves us with features a father leading his son into a vivid sunrise as a bass jumps out into the morning mist. Nick trails his hand in the water "which felt warm in the sharp chill of the morning ... and [he] felt quite sure that he would never die."

Hemingway's mastery of the fundamentals is also notably evident in "Up in Michigan," a story that differs in many ways from "Hills Like White Elephants" in both language and tone. Drawn from Hemingway's experiences hunting and fishing with his father in Michigan's Upper Peninsula, the narrator of "Up in Michigan" serves as the filter through which all information must pass. The narrator does not participate in the action of the story, and his voice is controlled, reportorial, and detached. Technically, he is an "omniscient narrator," meaning that he is authorized to enter the thought processes of his characters as thoroughly as he deems necessary. If the author provides his narrator access to the thoughts of a single character, that would be identified as "limited (or restricted) omniscient." That designation broadens to "unrestricted omniscient" when the narrator can access the thoughts of more than a single person. "Up in Michigan" is primarily the former: most of the interior glances the narrator provides concern Liz Coates. Only occasionally does the interior window expand to the object of Liz's emotional interest, Jim Gilmore, about whom we are informed that, at a drinking party, he "began to feel great" and that he "loved the taste and the feel of the whiskey." But the few thoughts of Jim's that we are provided don't help us fill in the motive for why, at the story's apex, he forces himself upon Liz. How does he perceive Liz? "He noticed that her hair was always neat behind ... He liked her face because it was so jolly but he never thought about her." Because of the point of view restrictions, we are privy to very little else about Jim as deducible from his point of view. The revelations about Liz based on what the narrator reveals about her thoughts, however, provide a somewhat more dimensional profile.

The fourth paragraph consists, significantly, of a description of Hortons Bay: a main street off of which are five residences, a combination post office and general store, a blacksmith's shop that had been purchased by Jim, a Methodist church on one end of the town and a schoolhouse on the other. The disposition of buildings in Hortons Bay seems to suggest a harmony of parts, a microcosm of how balance should be maintained in any community: equal parts domesticity (the main street residences), honest labor (the blacksmith's shop), connection with the world beyond Horton's Bay (general store/post office), formal learning (the school), and faith (the church). But, as the narrative slowly develops, all is not balanced in Hortons Bay. Whatever notion of quaintness might be suggested from the narrator's initial (and rather superficial) descriptions of the physical environs—"the sandy road"; "the big grove of elm trees"; "the bay blue and bright"; "the breeze blowing from Charlevoix and Lake Michigan" —evaporates as the story's point disturbingly takes shape. Rather than quaint, the descriptor "violent" would seem to apply since what bespeaks the essential quality of Hortons Bay is a behavior that would shame any community. In the aftermath of a drunken dinner party—itself the aftermath of a bloody deer hunt—a woman is raped by a member of that community. Where, one might ask, are the forces of church, school, and local business to counteract the crass characterization of Hortons Bay the final scenes leave us with?

When Jim arrives in Hortons Bay, he immediately becomes part of Liz's idealized world. Jim is a dream ideal and her thoughts and actions reflect a circumstance within which she and Jim might sometime in the near future begin a courtship to end in marriage. If Jim were of a similar emotional make-up, his thoughts about and actions toward Liz would—in his own way—complement hers. But there are no bouquets and no long walks on the lake front on Jim's agenda; certainly there are civil conversational exchanges between them, but nothing more.

Jim's indifference toward Liz is contrasted with her infatuation with him—although the word "love" has not yet entered her vocabulary. The third paragraph employs the rhetorical device of repetition to emphasize Liz's developing affection for Jim. A form of the word *like* appears nine times in a brief space that begins with the sentence, "Liz liked Jim very much." But "like" is a significant emotional distance from "love," and both would, for Jim, translate into "sex."

The narrator is trying to characterize the emotions of an inexperienced young woman who is struggling to comprehend where her thoughts are leading her. No romantic history about Liz is made available to us, but she senses that Jim's constant presence in her thoughts must mean that she has more than a passing affection for him. She is startled to find herself thinking about the black hair on his arms as he uses the wash basin, and how white those arms were "above the tanned line."

To this point, and for several more paragraphs, there is no dialogue. The narrator develops the plot mostly by straightforward description, deviating only in the subtle suggestions he makes regarding the intensity of Liz's interest in Jim. When Jim, D. J. Smith, and a couple of local men take a week off to go into the woods to hunt deer, Liz is depicted as almost frantic as she awaits Jim's return.

In a story this brief (6 pages long) and with a subject so intense (Jim rapes Liz in a shed by the lake) Hemingway's skills at writing compressed prose so clear there is no mistaking what the unstated implies are on display less than ten years after he had made the break from journalism to fiction writing.

On the subject of the credibility of Hemingway's characters, we will want to know whether Jim's violent behavior on the night of the assault has been in any way foreshadowed.

Good writers typically drop hints about how their characters will behave in later situations.

Jim is a physical being in a rugged environment, and he seems happiest when off on a hunting trip or debriefing about it afterward. He is savvy enough to interpret the signs Liz is giving off, even if their conversational exchanges have been minimal. While Liz is not particularly good at hiding her infatuation with Jim, she, in her "neatness," likely does not have a sixth sense about Jim's unforgivable intentions. Forces such as these make for a perfect storm of violence. The "stage clears," with extraneous characters exiting as Liz, who is pretending to read a book, is pulled from her thoughts of a conflicted courtship into the actions of an assault. She simply wants to stay up so that she can see Jim come through the living room and "take the way he looked up to bed with her." But Jim invites her to go outside. Haltingly, she accepts his invitation, and her dreams of a patient, tender courtship quickly disintegrate. Hemingway selects images consonant with that disillusionment in his short but pointed closing paragraphs: "There was no moon"; "the point was dark across the bay"; "the boards were hard ... and splintery"; "he had hurt her"; "A cold mist was coming up through the woods from the bay"; and, finally, for Liz, "everything felt gone." The description of the rape is uncharacteristically explicit for the 1920s, and it indicates how uncomfortable Hemingway must have been with those fictions where he was forced to sanitize the frank language ("vigorous English") that even the *Star* style guide knew was needed.

During his short tenure at the *Star*, Hemingway learned how to control what was being reported and how that reporting ought to be managed. In "Up in Michigan" Hemingway's application and control of these lessons is extraordinary. The rape scene is all the more disturbing because we are left to imagine some of the particulars. In theatrical terminology, that terrible concluding scene between Liz and Jim is known as the "scene a faire"—the obligatory scene that ties up all that came before, the scene that must occur in order for the narrative to succeed. And while Hemingway perfectly underplays the details that ought to be underplayed at the story's end, the true testament to "Up in Michigan," is this: the ending has been set up with such skill that the audience would still "get it" if Hemingway had terminated his narration when Jim whispers to Liz, "Come on for a walk."

Rule #3

Eliminate every superfluous word.

Chapter Three

Chekhov's Gun and Creative Sustainability

Tales about how a literary master developed his or her style are frequently apocryphal, but even half-truths can have their value. Thomas Mann is said to have set down 5,000 words every day of his writing life, then revised what he had written until he'd pared the original output down to 500 usable words. Dr. Johnson said that "good reading is precious hard writing." Every writer who has a prayer of succeeding eventually realizes that magic is manufactured, not bestowed. In this regard, Hemingway's history speaks for itself.

Perhaps it was the rigid discipline imposed upon young Hemingway by his parents, teachers, and early employers that disposed him to work hard at everything he did, and made him so contemptuous of individuals who were not similarly committed. His reading and research were as prodigious as they were pragmatic.

Like most authors, he worried about his ability to repeat the success of the novel that brought him first and optimal acclaim—for him it was *The Sun Also Rises*. But an appraisal of his work proves that Hemingway is one of the few writers who have assimilated a style so thoroughly and effectively that everything they write becomes suffused with that feature. The term *style* is frequently used interchangeably with *technique*. Used here, *style* is the parent of *technique*; it is the sum of techniques—the faithful absorption of each technique and how effectively they are brought together may result in a signature style. It is akin to the baseball pitcher who, ultimately, is affected by his arm strength, his ability to manipulate the seams on the baseball, his adroitness when fielding his position, and how effective he is pitching from the "stretch" when runners are on base. Overall mastery comes when one has both the ability and work ethic to incorporate each technique, an integration that provides the resulting performance with intrinsic merit and longevity.

While psychological factors would eventually cause Hemingway to doubt his ability to produce work that was on par with the revolutionary compositions of his early period, the consistent quality of his output over three decades provides evidence that the ability to compose brilliant prose can be attained and *is* sustainable. Hemingway was fortunate to be visited by the muse early in life, but his hard work and strong desire to learn caused her to stick around.

The novel that is justly rated as his best is *The Sun Also Rises*. Told from the first-person point of view of Jake Barnes, the novel provides multiple characters with fascinating backstories, the most intriguing of which belongs to Barnes himself. To test the integrity of any book, aspiring novelists might ask: What chapter, passage, character, or subplot could be eliminated from—or elaborated upon—that would result in a more effective product? None is the answer in *The Sun Also Rises*, a conclusion supported by the large majority of scholars who grant that, even in the opening chapters where it seems odd that Robert Cohn is receiving so much attention, there is a logic for that emphasis. Cohn represents the worst that the new century has to offer: he is selfish, unreliable, and whiny. But his presence and considerable shortcomings allow Hemingway to emphasize the value of individuals who, though not perfect themselves, have a sense of what is right, understand what friendship is, are not afraid of adversity, and, in fact, face it with grace and courage.

Again, the disciplined usage he learned to value during his time at the *Kansas City Star* allows *The Sun Also Rises* to soar, and its instant popularity in both America and Europe is testimony that he had landed upon an attractive approach, both in what he wrote about and in how he wrote about it. As his training dictated, Hemingway put all his focus on the surface narrative in *The Sun Also Rises*, and the attention paid to themes directly addressed in the novel was not a surprise to Hemingway. What did surprise him was what critics began to say about the significances that lay beneath the main story line, providing proof that his decision to let other themes, symbols, and messages bubble up in his fiction was in fact the correct one.

Russian playwright and short story writer Anton Chekhov was an early Modernist, concerned with finding means of expression that were an alternative to the war epics and aristocratic sagas that characterized fiction during the Tsarist regimes. Prompted to try his hand at short stories following the success of the plays he composed in his 20s, Chekhov was determined to write succinctly and with maximum clarity. In an experience that recalls the fortunate encounter Hemingway had with the editorial staff of the *Star* and their cherished house style, Chekhov was sent a note by a prominent Russian literary critic, Dmitry Grigorovich, ostensibly complimenting him on one of his early stories, "The Huntsman." "You have *real* talent, a talent that places you in the front rank among writers in the new generation," wrote Grigorovich. He appended his note with the suggestion that Chekhov "write less" and concentrate more on quality. Chekhov immediately saw the wisdom in the admonition:

"I have written my stories the way reporters write up their notes about fires—mechanically, half-consciously, caring nothing about either the reader or myself." So completely did Chekhov commit himself to trimming excesses and digressions from his prose that his disciples named a dramatic principle after him: "Chekhov's gun." No action or personage or object that appears in a drama or is described in a short story should remain if that action, personage, or object is not made use of later on in the narrative. In Chekhov's own words, "Remove everything that has no relevance to the story. If you say in the first chapter that there is a rifle hanging on the wall, in the second or third chapter it absolutely must go off. If it's not going to be fired, it shouldn't be hanging there."

Those who go to Chekov expecting a compressed style that parallels Hemingway's, however, will be disappointed. An average Chekhov sentence is substantially longer than the typical Hemingway sentence. But compression is not only measurable by word counts. A writer knows what *can* be said about a sunset, or what their protagonist wore to the induction ceremony, but what is their sensibility about what *must* or *should* be said? Every art form under the heading "Modern" was obliged to consider the benefits of reduction, of trimming an object or message to its core while taking care not to strip it of the trappings that made it what it was. In writing, the suggestive nature of compressed prose can sometimes have more impact than explicatory prose. Using words directly and frugally—where ideas are transmitted literally—is one mode of communication; using a word or words chosen for the "picture" they supply our imagination, or the idea suggested by those words, is another. In either mode, the writer is acknowledging the power of reduction. Regarding suggestive writing, Chekhov remarked, "Don't tell me the moon is shining; show me the glint of light on broken glass."

The most effective writers of prose are capable of such fresh and lyrical phrasing that their work has an effect similar to poetry. Page after page of James Joyce's fiction reads like poetry. The same can be said of the lyrical feel of passages from Proust, Faulkner, Thomas Wolfe, Porter, and Hemingway. In *The Sun Also Rises,* this lyricism comes when Bill Gorton and Jake Barnes temporarily escape the dirt, dust, and moral corruption of Pamplona and travel into the Pyrenees to fish the ice-cold Irati River. Placed in an idyllic setting, their long-time unqualified friendship unwinds into loose and frank conversation. Each can reveal to the other, without equivocation, information of the most intimate sort. Against a backdrop of water purling over smooth rock, trout leaping in the sunlight, wine chilled in the river and imbibed almost sacramentally, their dialogue takes on a lyrical quality.

After a glorious hour of fishing—each in a separate spot he thinks will be most productive—they reconvene at a designated location on the riverbank. The talk is about fishing, but what constitutes true friendship is the primary concern of the exchange:

"Get any? [Bill] asked. He had his rod and his bag and his net all in one hand, and he was sweating. I hadn't heard him come up because of the noise from the dam.

"Six. What did you get?

Bill sat down, opened up his bag, laid a big trout on the grass. He took out three more, each one a little bigger than the last, and laid them side by side in the shade from the tree. His face was sweaty and happy.

"How are yours?"

"Smaller."

"Let's see them."

"They're packed."

"How big are they really?"

"They're all about the size of your smallest."

"You're not holding out on me?"

"I wish I were."

"Get them all on worms?"

"Yes."

"You lazy bum!"

This banter is not just filler. As they unwrap their lunch and continue to kid one another, the conversation becomes a word association game that only those who are familiar with each other can compete in. Starting with what the hard-boiled eggs taste like, Jake and Bill segue into a humorous existential discussion ("Which came first, the chicken or the egg?"), then to a topic current in the newspapers of the time, the Scopes Trial and William Jennings Bryan's naivete about evolution, and finally to a segment in which they celebrate being together in this "sacred" place.

Sensing the trap lying in a conversational exchange that could logically culminate in a sappy profession of mutual affection, Hemingway sidesteps the snare by reviving the humor of the occasion, satirizing Catholic ritual during a discussion of the delights of drinking wine. The language of ceremony "consecrates." The wine is kept cool by its immersion in the pure water of the river. Following the lighthearted mockery, the mood turns solemn and silent, and Jake, peaceful and serious, can speak candidly with Bill about his love for Lady Brett Ashley. Here, as in so many places in this novel, Hemingway lets the intention of his prose determine his descriptive strategy, allowing him to avoid being sappy or sentimental during the sensitive exchange between the two friends.

By the time the American edition of *The Sun Also Rises* was published, Hemingway had established both the good writing and the bad lifestyle habits that would remain for the rest of his life. He learned them both at the *Kansas City Star*. What began in high school as a larkish routine of tippling hard cider with his friend, Bill Smith, evolved into more regular bouts of drinking wine, which he decided "was a more worldly drink," in Kansas City. His drinking companion became Ted Brumback, a newly hired reporter for the *Star* who had attended Cornell for three years before spending four months driving ambulances in France as part of the American Field Service. "As it did for many Americans in the twenties, drinking possessed a special excitement" for Hemingway. In 1927, Hemingway wrote to his mother, "I have never been a drunk nor even a steady drinker (You will hear legends that I am ... they are tacked on everyone that ever wrote about people who drink)," but there is much evidence to the contrary. In a letter to Charles Scribner he says, "Don't worry about the words. I've been doing that since 1921. I always count them when I knock off and am drinking the first whiskey and soda." His friend and hunting companion, Buck Lanham, described Hemingway's drinking habits in 1949: "Although he takes handfuls of sleeping pills, he always wakes up around four-thirty in the morning. He usually starts drinking right away and writes standing up, with a pencil in one hand and a drink in the other."

But the good writing habits weathered the torrent of liquor. The environment at the *Star* was severe, but it allowed Hemingway to understand that he had much to learn. Asked by George Plimpton, in his capacity as the editor of *The Paris Review*, whether newspaper writing was good preparation for a young writer, Hemingway replied, "On *The Star* you were forced to write a good declarative sentence.

This is useful to anyone. Newspaper work will not harm a young writer and could help him if he gets out of it in time." What did Hemingway mean by getting out in time? Newspaper writing is a niche skill, with parameters imposed by the purpose and very nature of a newspaper. When those constraints are so inflexible that only fact-gathering and colorless, unnuanced recapitulation are allowed, the damage to a young writer's imagination could be serious. As much as Hemingway applauded what the newspaper and its rules did for him, he was wise enough to take what was useful, ignore what wasn't, and know when to move on.

When advised by John Dos Passos to "get the weather in your god-damned book—weather is very important," Dos Passos was really saying that Hemingway, now a novelist instead of a newspaper reporter, needed to use his imagination. He was now required to *invent* situations, places, and characters when actual experience fell short. When it was going well for Hemingway, he would lose himself in the world he had conjured up: "Some days it went so well," he wrote, "that you could make the country so that you could walk into it through the timber to come out into the clearing and work up onto the high ground and see the hills beyond the arm of the lake."

Hemingway loved to put himself in the path of harm so that he could cull experiential material for his fiction. But whenever he needed to fill a space, his vivid imagination was there to assist. Much about *The Sun Also Rises* is based on his own experiences. Fiction that relies mainly on a foundation of reality is known as a "roman à clef," or "narrative with a key." The key is the connection the fictional characters, settings, and situations have to their counterparts in reality. In *The Sun Also Rises*, every character—from Robert Cohn to the bullfighter Pedro Romero—was based on people Hemingway had met during his adventures. Major locations in which actions

"If a writer of prose knows enough about what he is writing about, he may omit things that he knows... The dignity of movement of an iceberg is due to only one eighth of it being above water."

— From Death in the Afternoon

are set—Paris, Pamplona, the Pyrenees, and San Sebastian—were places Hemingway knew well. While it is difficult to know with absolute certainty which of the situations dramatized in the book were "lived," which were amalgamations of several experiences, and which were invented completely, biographical research suggests that the book's plot and subplots rcflcct conflicts whosc actuality can be verified. Hemingway does try to disguise references to real people, but because he is so fascinated by his depictions of how his acquaintances look and act, he is usually not successful. In a 1953 letter to his lawyer, Alfred Rice, regarding a sketch he was working on, Hemingway notes, "Most of the people in this story are alive and I was writing it very carefully to not have anybody identifiable." Occasionally, he admitted that he simply went ahead and used real names and situations: "I put in Dick Boulton and Billy Tabeshaw as real people with their real names because it was pretty sure they would never read the *Transatlantic Review*."

Hemingway had plenty of opportunities to exercise his imagination in his writing. But he did have limits regarding certain people, places, and experiences, with his hometown of Oak Park, Illinois, proving the most out-of-bounds subject. In a 1952 letter to his friend Charles Fenton, he confessed, "I had a wonderful novel to write about Oak Park and would never do it because I did not want to hurt living people. I did not think that a man should make money out of his father shooting himself nor out of his mother who drove him to it." He adds, "When I started I wrote some short stories about actual things and two of them hurt people. I felt bad about it. Later if I used actual people I used only those for whom I had completely lost respect and then I tried to give them a fair shake."

As noted previously, the first two chapters of *The Sun Also Rises* present a narrator who—for reasons that become clear later on—

feels a need to disparage the Princeton-educated Robert Cohn. If amount of coverage is a measure of importance, Cohn should be a main or pivotal figure in the events to follow. But Cohn's prominence is short-lived. He is important only as a "set-up" device—as someone whose personality is antithetical to those characters who do turn out to be vital to the plot. Cohn represents attitudes and behaviors that run counter to those of the novel's more principled characters: Jake Barnes, Lady Brett Ashley, and Bill Gorton, who take the stage in Chapters 3 through 6. Cohn is a "bad drunk" who gets so carried away during his drinking bouts that he must resort to physical violence, thus embarrassing "the good drunks," Jake, Brett, and Bill. Cohn is a coward, a whiner, and an equivocator—someone who is clearly not, to use Brett's phrase, "one of us." Because of this, he is shunted into the background once his role as foil has been established. He does reappear, but his reappearance is always to remind readers of a type that Jake, and Hemingway, can't abide.

A central theme of the novel is generally good people struggling to cope with a rapidly changing and not-always-hospitable world. Jake, Bill, and Brett are united in that struggle, and Paris, as the center of all things intellectual and artistic, is necessarily the *nexus* of such existential crises. All of the resources are there, as are all of the people who might be able to give Jake and his coterie of lost souls some direction. Instead, in what seems like a particularly masochistic decision, the entourage—including the unwelcome Cohn—decamps for Pamplona and the hedonism of the Fiesta de San Fermin. To emphasize the moral corruption of this phase of Jake's search, a sentence at the beginning of Chapter 15 reads, "San Fermin is *also* a religious festival." The themes that emerge from this sequence of chapters are dissolution (not a scene goes by without someone drinking to excess), perfidy (Jake learns Cohn has gone behind his back and slept with Brett), pimping (Jake ignores his longtime friendship with Montoya, the innkeeper and fellow bullfighting aficionado, when he introduces bullfighting prodigy Pedro Romero to Brett), and hypocrisy (Jake and Brett have the temerity to visit a Catholic church during this debauch). Even when exiled to the background, Cohn justifies the attention Jake pays him in the first two chapters and proves himself the lowest of the low—sycophant, braggart, and coward—before he is finally excised from the group.

In the novel's final chapter, Jake's trip back to Paris is delayed when he decides to stop in the coastal city of San Sebastian. His movements there, and the upbeat nature of his language, suggest that he might have found philosophical equanimity after all. Purged of Cohn, no longer responsible for Brett (who has run off with Pedro Romero), free from the dust and general befoulment of Pamplona, cleansed physically and perhaps even spiritually after a swim in the Bay of Biscay, Jake believes that he has risen from his personal hell. But Hemingway's overriding thesis is that, in these cynical times, with the horrors of World War I still so firmly embedded in the world's consciousness, there is no redemption for the Lost Generation. Accordingly, Jake's peace is shattered by Brett, who once more pulls him into her orbit when she finds herself in Madrid, in desperate need of rescue.

Although Hemingway's characters do a good deal of roaming as they search for meaning, *The Sun Also Rises* is anything but loose in organization, execution, and theme. It is often cited as the fictional equivalent to the poetry of William Carlos Williams, the precisionist drama of Samuel Becket, the stark sculpture of Alberto Giacometti, and the paintings of Pablo Picasso or Georges Braque. It has been credited as the definitive statement of the Modernist movement. In so many ways, the novel taps into the Modernist mind at work:

challenging conventional concepts of organization and execution at every juncture; accepting of the oblique; the theme of impotence; the paucity—yet sufficiency—of descriptive detail; the use of extended dialogue to augment the movement of the plot; symbolism on both micro- and macrocosmic levels; and the courage to place the existential crisis of a deeply flawed main character, Jake, in the foreground.

By 1925, still quite young and carrying with him the influences that had supported his early writings, Hemingway had evolved into the kind of writer he himself would have praised (and *did*, as per his substantial ego). Without abandoning the precept to compose compressed paragraphs he'd learned at the *Star*, Hemingway was also able to anticipate literature and the art world adjusting to the groundswell of Modernist innovation regarding form and content.

There is some humor in all of this. A story circulates about Hemingway, the reporter, testing the rules of the *Star* guide—and the patience of his editor—when he attempted to sneak a paragraph or two of the verboten "expressionistic" prose into his stories. We can only wonder about the reaction of the editor who came across those passages—and the reprimand that followed.

The assignment was to cover a traffic accident in downtown Kansas City, a simple enough occurrence that Hemingway elected to expand into a psychological profile of a cousin of the driver of the offending vehicle. The interview—as dramatized as it was tangential to the actual motor vehicle accident—was conducted at a bar on the outskirts of the city.

Rule #4

Try to preserve the atmosphere of the speech in your quotation.

Chapter Four

"You Talkin' to Me?"
The Voice-Address Relationship

We've already looked at the effort Hemingway put into generating narratives that are innovative, active, shorn of verbal excesses, and structurally sound. With very few exceptions, in their final, edited form, his books attain a level of excellence that has kept them on bookshelves around the world for almost a century. Firmly inscribed in his mind was the type of individual he wanted his prose to reach, the same audience that read and appreciated the works Hemingway himself respected—works by Joyce, Turgenev, Virginia Woolf, Joseph Conrad, Dostoevsky, Marcel Proust, Anderson, Tolstoy, and Dickens. But his work also appealed to readers well beyond the ivory towers of academia and the salons being conducted in urban bohemias. Average people found that he spoke their language and shared their concerns, from abortion and cowardice to ambition, hypocrisy, and suicide. With Hemingway, they did not have to think about what they were reading; instead, they could fall into any of his narratives because they recognized and felt the words he had chosen.

A writer's voice contains every single element she invests a project with, from the explicit to the subtle; it is the authority that commands the reader to continue on. Sometimes the subtleties are difficult to pinpoint, and we are compelled to resort to the visceral (i.e., "I simply liked the way it was done!"), but there are legions of scholars whose lives are spent trying to outline those subtleties.

The equation is simple. Either a writer establishes a distinctive voice, or the reader will not be disposed to accept a thesis posited, a plot initiated, or a scene set. Most writers don't keep at the craft long enough to develop that voice and gain an understanding of what it means to tap into their "internal author." Writing well can be as natural as breathing, and somewhere within us all is that natural voice, a voice that is the equivalent of a smile directed at someone we care deeply about. The authority of Hemingway's narrative voice secures our attention and disposes us to buy into the experience he is about to relate.

But not everyone has the time, or the desire, to devote to finding and inhabiting a writing voice such as the one Hemingway worked on so assiduously during his youth. If you are speaking or writing casually and not thinking seriously about becoming a professional writer, you likely aren't too concerned with type and consistency of voice. But perhaps you should be. Most informal writing—the email to a friend, the quip posted on social media, the cover letter to a prospective employer—is still accompanied by the wish that the message be conveyed as fully in meaning and tone as it can be. With a minimal amount of conscientiousness, even simple communication—*phatic speech*, the basic exchanges that keep the lines of communications open—can generate a valid, individualized voice. Like it or not, our writer's voice, our compositional personality, is front and center when we write to an audience. Any audience. The average reader looks between and beneath the lines for verification that what they are reading is coming from a legitimate source. Our fraud and phoniness detectors work full-time; most of us have a good sense of when we are being conned.

In contexts where the search for a viable writing voice is serious business, the advice given in any composition course is that a writing voice should first be natural. The range of "natural voice" usage is broad. Natural here can be applied to the semi-formal voice Hemingway was compelled to assume by virtue of his job as a reporter—direct and unadorned. A discourse can be natural in formal research paper writing as long as the writer remains within the dictional, syntactic, and rhetorical parameters that characterize his occupation. Natural is a term that can even describe the discourse of a stand-up comedian. As with common discourse, familiarity with diction, syntax, style, and subject matter will point the user in the direction of a natural voice.

Grammar is the skill of using language correctly, rhetoric the art of using language effectively. Hemingway internalized the most sensible rules of the *Star*'s style sheet to the extent that good grammar (if not necessarily good spelling, which was a weakness) was present in everything he wrote. A similar algorithm applies to his absorption of those rhetorical devices originally designed to clarify speech. Function persists, but figurative speech, when used prudently, is also capable of providing one's writing voice a special dimension. Hemingway's exposure to the broad range of figuration gave him options which, in turn, resulted in his unique voice.

In letters and articles in which he discusses his own style, Hemingway rarely mentions technical aspects; rather, his remarks are mostly general and predictable, his responses tailored to what he believes interviewers want to hear. If it is true that Hemingway did not know precisely what a *scheme* is (it is a deliberate deviation in the way words and syllables are arranged in a sentence) or what a *trope* is (it is an intentional departure from the ordinary signification of a word), it is without a doubt that he had seen examples of *isocolon, asyndeton, anastrophe, chiasmus, epanalepsis*, and *asyndeton* in his reading, and had used variations of those devices in his writing. Two rather obvious pieces of advice for new writers typify how spot-on but non-technical his advice could be. From an interview in *By-Line* on how a writer trains himself to register important facts gleaned from reality, he says, "Find what gave you the emotion; what the action was that gave you the excitement. Then write it down making it clear so the reader will see it too and have the same feeling that you had." In the same interview, he argues, "You should be able to go into a room and when you come out know everything you saw there and not only that. If that room gave you any feeling you should know exactly what it was that gave you that feeling." They are not exactly the most focused or most inspiring pieces of advice, but his own writing had more to do with instinct than instruction, with hard practice than theory. Those interested in learning from the master are better off going directly to his stories and taking note of the specific qualities that make the writing so compelling.

Direct style is not necessarily simple, and it is incorrect to attach the pejorative word "simplistic" to Hemingway's prose. His dominant use of simple and compound sentences in descriptive paragraphs and in dialogue indicates that his ear was always attuned to how people truly spoke. What stands out as vitiating the pith and power of his straightforward language is the ban against profanity that Hemingway and his publishers had to contend with. With the Comstock Act of 1873 equating profanity with obscenity in literature, linguistic verisimilitude was impossible for most of Hemingway's writing life. His strongest epithets—profanity whittled down to curses—were no substitute for what he knew needed to be captured on the page.

Otherwise, Hemingway showed his sophistication as a stylist by using rhetorical license to flex his expression as needed. From time to time in his dialogue he would invent a word or use a known word in an unconventional way. In *The Sun Also Rises* he plays with the word "utilize" ("Let us utilize the birds of the air") in his and Bill's mocking of the rituals of the Catholic Church, instead of using the less pretentious form, "use." Occasionally, he will coin a term, most frequently in conversational discourse, where regular people do in fact invent new usages. In "The Snows of Kilimanjaro," he has the dying Harry respond to his wife's calling him a coward by asking her, "What's the use of slanging me?"

Irony is present throughout the exchange between Harry and his wife, Helen. Their marriage is failing and he is in the awkward position of knowing that he may possibly die before he will be able to "best" Helen in setting the terms of their divorce. It isn't far into their exchanges before we realize that him telling her that he loves her actually means the opposite. Hemingway, via Harry, uses *metonymy* (the substitution of some attribute(s) for what is meant) when he refers to her social class as "Old Westbury, Saratoga, Palm Beach." Of course he employs simple metaphor (of the type simile): "snow as smooth to see as cake frosting and light as powder." Harry says, "Love is a dunghill, and I'm the cock that gets on it to crow" and, later, "Your damned money was my armour." Harry also "slipped into the familiar lie he made his bread and butter by." When he says to his wife, "I'd like to destroy you a few times in bed," he is using *periphrasis*, meaning a phrase that "hovers around" something that could be said more directly; it is a linguistic evasion, like circumlocution. Personification occurs toward the conclusion of the story with "He had just felt death come by again ... [It] rested its head on the foot of the cot and he could smell its breath."

The speaker in this story is a nonparticipatory, third-person narrator who has "limited" omniscience in that he reports on Harry's actions and innermost thoughts. The narrator reports on Helen's actions, but further information about Helen is limited to Harry's observations of her. We can only infer what she is thinking and feeling on the basis of what she says when engaged with her husband or the safari leader. Hemingway elects to add a dimension to what is revealed about Harry in the italicized sections where, presumably, Harry is either half-conscious or dreaming in his sleep. We can deduce that Harry is a miserable individual by the way he talks to Helen. That conclusion is corroborated in the dream sequences, where he discloses more that is disturbing about himself. He is an inveterate liar, marries wealthy women for what they can do for his reputation as a lady-killer, and is a failed writer who has talked about writing all his life but never had the courage or self-discipline to actually sit down and do it. He excoriates friends such as "Julian"—F. Scott Fitzgerald in the real world—for their infatuation with wealth and wealthy people, which ultimately wrecked their careers. But, by his own admission, Harry knows that he is not much better than Julian.

Hemingway would not be the best person to consult on the mechanical specifics of establishing a credible, interesting, and consistent voice in writing. His own voice generated working discourse, not theories of discoursing. He recognized that thinking too hard about formal technique could be a major stumbling block in producing text.

Like most writers he had his quirks, even superstitions about getting started, getting back to work, and making sure the voice he had spent so long cultivating never became compromised. In *A Moveable Feast* he writes about not being able to write:

Sometimes when I was starting a new story and could not get it going I would sit in front of the fire and squeeze the peel of the little oranges into the edge of the flame and watch the sputter of blue that they made. I would stand and look out over the roofs of Paris and think, "Do not worry. You always have written before and you will write now. All you have to do is write one true sentence. Write the truest sentence that you know." So finally I would write one true sentence, and then go on from there. It was easy then because there was always one true sentence that I knew or had seen or had heard someone say. If I started to write elaborately, or like someone introducing or presenting something, I found that I could cut that scrollwork or ornament out and throw it away and start with the first true simple declarative sentence I had written.

Hallmarks of the best writing in any genre—including newspaper accounts—are an attention-grabbing introduction and an even more compelling conclusion, or "kicker," in newsroom speak. Hemingway's ability to conclude with special gusto reveals a writer who knew the importance of sustaining creative energy to the end.

The set-up in "Kilimanjaro" is such that we are mainly interested in the thought process of Harry as he faces his mortality. The story is a paradigm of the importance of singularity of purpose in a narrative; nothing in the tale—in the descriptive passages, in the dialogue, in the flashback sequences—is unrelated to Harry's imminent death. Hemingway's point of view ought to be third-person omniscient—and it is. Analyzing the voice of the speaker—who approximates Harry's voice while remaining in the third-person mode—gives us volumes of information to characterize Harry with. While Hemingway gives us an individual who is generally bitchy and cruel, we are also reminded that Harry's thinking is in a highly accelerated mode: he is about to die. In the interest of keeping the focus where it should be, Hemingway wisely keeps his narrator muted for the most part; a majority of the discourse leading up to the first italicized flashback is dialogue that features Harry finding different ways to bait and taunt Helen. The pace of the dialogue is frantic, befitting Harry's need to say things, both good and bad, before his time runs out. When we come to the voice that covers the flashbacks, the pace diminishes; we have time to process what the past has meant to Harry, time to qualify our assessment of his character, and to determine if any reassessment is warranted. What results is a picture of Harry that should mitigate any harsh judgments of him. For his war experiences, he earns our respect; for his foolishness in gambling away all his money, he deserves no compassion. He shows loyalty to his male friends but cruelty to female conquests. His thinking back to his childhood and recounting some of his early disappointments with his family elicits our sympathy, and we try to commiserate with his plans to write about the war, encounters with death, relationships with women, and the loss of "the Paris that he cared about," but we are held back, recalling that Hemingway had nothing but disdain for would-be writers whose resolve ultimately amounted to nothing.

The closing paragraphs of "Kilimanjaro" join the two modes of consciousness present in the story, and present the reader with a challenge. As the morning light comes on, the night-long howl of the hyena begins to subside. The pain from Harry's gangrenous leg has subsided; or perhaps he is only dreaming that it has. He comments to Helen, who is either there and half-listening or another construct of his imagination, "I'm getting as bored with dying as everything else." Then come the observations on death that seem directed either to no one or directly to death, which he feels approaching and tells to go away. Harry's observations that "It was morning and had been morning for some time" and that he had "heard the plane," only

"Find what gave you the emotion; what the action was that gave you the excitement. Then write it down making it clear so the reader will see it too and have the same feeling that you had."

— From Monologue to the Maestro

make sense as hallucinations. Similarly, we are skeptical about the occurrence of a conversation between Harry and the plane's pilot, and about the flight itself as the rising aircraft banks over Kilimanjaro, the mythical burial ground of the mysterious leopard. Harry and pilot "Compie" pass through a darkened sky and a rainstorm, then into the light. They view the square top of the mountain and, suddenly, Harry "knew that there was where he was going."

Except for the brief closing scene in which Helen sees Harry still on his cot, now dead, the ending has an interesting consonance to Tolstoy's story "The Death of Ivan Ilych." Hemingway read many of the Russian writers. He wrote of being influenced by Dostoevsky (*The Brothers Karamazov*), Turgenev ("all" of what he wrote), and Chekhov. But at the top of the list was Tolstoy. While there is no explicit evidence that Hemingway had read "The Death of Ivan Ilych," several points of similarity suggest that he likely held deep admiration for the story. Like Harry, Justice Ilych is in the final stages of a fatal disease. Bedridden as Harry is "cot-ridden," Ilych, in constant pain, fades in and out of consciousness. We are privy to the particulars of his dreams, which center on his regrets that he wasn't a more loving father and that he has been such a materialist. Likewise, Harry's dreams are dotted with painful recollections of poor judgment and past bad behavior. The most persuasive argument that Hemingway appropriated from the Russian tale revolves around the shared existential themes. We don't know the specific destination of the plane carrying Harry and his pilot, but the language describing the event seems exhilarative; nor do we know what kind of environment Ivan enters when he passes through the dark tunnel and "into the light," but the language here is also ethereal.

Though he never embraced its philosophy, Hemingway had a lifelong fascination with the rituals of the Catholic Church, and with the possibilities of redemption in the afterlife. Tolstoy, too, embraced a version of Christianity ("anarchist-pacifist"), which included a rejection of aristocratic values and a belief in an afterlife. The positive imaging at the conclusion of both stories—Harry's view of Kilimanjaro "as wide as all the world" and Ivan's "in place of death there was life"—isn't enough to suggest that Hemingway was directly playing off another writer's theme and situation, but the general point might be that—entirely properly and without at all coming near the very dangerous border of plagiarism—this is what writers do.

An African safari, an unhappy couple, a frustrated writer, an end-of-story fatality—sounds very familiar. And, while there are thematic similarities between "The Short Happy Life of Francis Macomber" and "The Snows of Kilimanjaro," writers interested in voice-related concerns will want to focus on the former. What the story required was different from what "Kilimanjaro" needed. "Kilimanjaro" was Harry's story; "Macomber" is only partially about Francis Macomber's personality and behavior on safari. Not only are readers focused on the reactions to Macomber's behavior, they're also curious about the reactions of others in the party, and even—since the story invites us to consider the limits of point of view—the reactions of certain wounded animals.

The functional part of the story entails both Francis's initial act of cowardice with the wounded lion and his "reclamation" action with the water buffalo. But the incidents don't occur in a vacuum. There are other people present, people whose reactions are important to the narrator as he passes both formative and terminal judgments on Francis. What the situation necessitates, then, is a broader perspective that can provide insight into a range of reactions.

Unless there are multiple authors of a text (which always presents a problem in establishing one voice), there is a single voice that transcends all others present in a work. That voice belongs to

"If you describe someone it is flat, as a photograph is, and from my standpoint a failure. If you make him up from what you know, there should be all the dimensions."

— From The Art of Fiction: Ernest Hemingway

the author. In a story with characters who engage in dialogue or who speak out in some other form (as in a speech or a soliloquy), the author has the dual obligation of investing his narrator's voice with authority and consistency and being certain that, as he "enters" the voice of others in his cast of characters, he does so with the authority and consistency that befits their role in the story.

As mentioned earlier in this chapter, a reader must be careful when identifying the various voices in a text. The short story "Haircut," by Hemingway's one-time favorite writer, Ring Lardner, is told from the first-person point of view of a barber who himself tells a story (within the story) about a traveling salesman whose cruelty is unmatched in the region. When he plays a particularly mean trick on a local boy with a severe learning disability, the barber relates the tale to his customers as if it were a comic skit. When the salesman himself becomes the victim of a retaliatory trick, one which costs him his life, the barber again fails to acknowledge that the man deserved the reprisal. The barber's refrain continues to be, "That Jim Kendall [the salesman]; he certainly was a card!" Such consistency is crucial to establishing voice.

The narrator in "Macomber" is omniscient. Since a major event has already taken place when the first exchange between the principals occurs, we are immediately able to pick up on the undercurrent of awkwardness in the conversation. Francis Macomber has outed himself as a coward, as he dropped his rifle and ran from a lion that he just shot and wounded. His wife, Margot, the safari guide, Robert Wilson, and an African mess boy are not doing a very good job disguising their disgust. The first sentence hints at the tension as the small group decides which beverage it will order for lunch, meanwhile "pretending that nothing had happened." Margot finds numerous ways to pick on her husband before saying, forthrightly,

"I wish it hadn't happened. Oh, I wish it hadn't happened." With the benefit of his omniscience, the narrator both tells us that Wilson doesn't care very much for Margot and places us inside his mind: "She wasn't stupid," [he] thought, "no, not stupid." Wilson simply detests Macomber's cowardice and, more so, Macomber's misguided attempts to persuade Wilson not to mention the incident back at the clubhouse. Omniscience, though it can see everything, must still be selective—a writer must decide which inner thoughts get aired. Clearly, it is reasonable to get the protagonist's reaction to his companions' admonishments:

Francis Macomber lay on his cot with the mosquito bar over him and listened to the night noises ... It was neither all over nor was it beginning. It was there exactly as it happened with some parts of it indelibly emphasized and he was miserably ashamed at it. But more than shame he felt cold, hollow fear in him.

When the narrator's attention turns to the lion, the limits of omniscience are tested. A flashback in Macomber's mind takes us back to the morning of the hunt. The flexibility of omniscience permits the narrator to close in on the movements of the lion in the high grass and its reaction to the "object," which is the vehicle used to pursue game.

The lion still stood majestically and coolly toward this object that his eyes only showed in silhouette, bulking like some super-rhino. There was no man smell carried toward him and he watched the object, moving his great head a little from side to side. Then watching the object, not afraid, but hesitating before going down the bank to drink with such a thing opposite him, he saw a man figure detach itself from it and he turned his heavy head and swung away toward the cover of the trees as he heard a cracking crash and felt the slam of a .30-06 220-gram bullet that bit his flank and ripped in sudden hot scalding nausea through his stomach.

The observation that the lion was "not afraid" taxes the allowable range of what the narrator can and cannot know. In the enthusiasm to represent the lion's perception in the moments prior to being shot, Hemingway used "poetic license" to articulate the lion's rather graphic sensations. His other justification was that he was—intentionally and therefore legitimately—using a figure of speech called *pathetic fallacy* in which natural objects, including animals, are spoken of as having human properties. Such a rendering occurs again in the story as, after the lion is wounded, he lies flat in the grass festering with "hatred," waiting to spring at Macomber. Though he rarely needs it, we can allow Hemingway some suspension of disbelief in situations where we might otherwise question the legitimacy of his technical choices.

The point needs to be restated here that Hemingway's skills as a writer of "properly grammatical and rhetorical" prose are always in evidence but were, like everything about his compositional habits, far more naturally than clinically derived. He simply loved the language and did his best to present it in a way that *felt* right to him. With just a few formal cues from his *Star* training to prod him along the way, he developed a sense of what could and could not be done with the English language within the confines of a story. Hemingway's guides to proper language usage were internal and intuitive, absorbed and assimilated on the fly as he lived and grew with the language.

Rule #5

Both simplicity and good taste suggest home rather than residence and lives rather than resides.

Chapter Five

Main Bout of the Evening: Descriptive Grammar versus Prescriptive Grammar

When the zeitgeist of the '60s and '70s indicated that grammar was malleable, English teachers around the United States, along with book, magazine, and newspaper editors, tried to lead a "back to the future" movement, believing that sticking a thumb or two in the dike would restore grammar to the strict discipline it had once been. Conscientious parents, who as students had been indoctrinated with the belief that if the rules of grammar collapsed the fall of the republic would soon follow, fretted about their children's grammatically unsound futures. Publishers of dictionaries attempted to block the trend toward relaxing the definitions of words and broadening the conditions for acceptable usage by spending outrageous sums of money looking for ways to tighten denotations so that the appearance of that book on bookshelves would signal that the last word on words and their meanings lay within. A number of dictionaries surfaced during those two tumultuous decades, including Random House's *New American Heritage Dictionary*, which was the putative, practical alternative to the authoritative but cumbersome *Oxford English Dictionary*.

But the dilemma was too deep to be resolved by a sleek new tome of prescriptions. The issues with any attempt to codify usage were identified by Jacques Derrida in his landmark *Of Grammatology*, where he presented a cogent thesis that "laws" governing aspects of language use—including definitions—were pointless since nothing about language is stable enough to be subject to such governance.

The Modernists popularized the concepts of pushing language to its limits and ignoring convention. In the crucible of their expressive experiments, these writers explored what might be possible for language. What Gertrude Stein tried to do with *The Making of Americans*, her "unbelievably long book," places her at one extreme of the experimental spectrum. Hemingway said that the book "went on endlessly in repetitions that a more conscientious writer would have put in the waste basket." Faulkner operated outside the lines of conventional narrative technique, but with study and an understanding of the Southern ethos that he represented, his fiction was accessible. Joyce plotted his own route through structure and meaning, and came out a genius on the other side. Symbolist fiction, derived from the French love affair with all things symbolic, elevated the narratives of Steinbeck, Porter, and Hemingway.

Whatever strictures are in play, meaning is at the mercy of the mechanics that make communication possible. From the beginning of Hemingway's training as a reporter, he was prudent enough to not endanger his job by flouting the *Star's* style sheet. He saw his future ultimately as a creative writer and not as a reporter, and it must have required considerable restraint for him to resist embellishing both syntax and meaning in his assignments. In time, though, he was able to persuade his editor to let him cover a specific beat and to add a human dimension to figures that typically would be written about in the plainest of plain prose. One of his beats was the emergency room of a Kansas City hospital.

Reflecting the era, the guide was—from Rule #1 to Rule #110—a prescriptive document. Any issues Hemingway might have had with it would not have centered on subject-verb agreement, tense consistency, adverbial positioning, or other fundamentals. Rather, the liberties he took once he was allowed to humanize his hospital articles were syntactic (pertaining to the interconnected parts of a sentence) and dictional (pertaining to the choice of words and how and where to use them). In January 1918, the first paragraph of one of his on-scene narratives, titled "At the End of the Ambulance Run," read:

> *The night ambulance attendants shuffled down the long, dark corridors at the General Hospital with an inert burden on the stretcher. They turned in at the receiving ward and lifted the unconscious man to the operating table. His hands were calloused and he was unkempt and ragged, a victim of a street brawl near the city market.*

The concision of the opening three sentences points to a reporter attempting to fall in line with the mandates of the *Star*'s style sheet. One can envision his editor both applauding the paragraph and asking the reporter which, among the 13 adjectives, could be excised without compromising what a reader needed to know about the incident. Does the word "ragged" really advance our picture of what the man was wearing (as sequences of descriptive words are supposed to do), or is "ragged" just a kind of unkemptness and, technically, a category overlap? Can a better word than "burden" be found following "inert"? Can one imagine something large enough to require being transported by "attendants" not being a "burden"?

In the same article, Hemingway reports on "an aged printer" coming in for treatment because lead had gotten into his bloodstream via a cut on his thumb; the surgeon announces that the finger will need to be amputated. The printer refuses, saying that it will make him unable to work, and he leaves. The article continues:

The French artist who vowed to commit suicide if he lost his right hand in battle might have understood the struggle the old man had alone in the darkness. Later that night the printer returned. He was very drunk. 'Just take the damn works, doc, take the whole damn works,' he wept.

Star editors would have been fine with punchy syntactic units such as "He was very drunk." But what about the three times he uses the lame phrase of address, "Why, doc!" (see page 114 for full article)? It's also unclear what Hemingway is trying to capture by using "he wept" as a speech indicator. Is the printer's weeping a separate action from him instructing the surgeon to "take the whole damn works?" Is his sentence one long weep? What does "the whole damn works" denote? The reference to the French artist who vows to commit suicide sounds literary, but we don't have nearly enough context to judge its propriety.

In the article's final paragraph, the tonal unevenness persists. Hemingway generalizes about cases coming into the ER at night. "The night shift," he says, "has a wider range of the life and death tragedy—and even comedy—of the city [than the day shift]." With the noun "comedy" being adjacent to the next phrase, "When 'George' comes in ..." it is natural to assume that there is something comic about George's arrival—but since the man is bloodied and broken on a stretcher, this could not be further from the mark, just as one would expect in a city hospital.

For a document that isn't especially systematic in organizing its precepts, the degree of influence the style sheet had on those devoted to their profession and to their newspaper must have derived from its almost mythic reputation. The newspaper office—when newspapers were truly the determiner of all that the public needed to know, in the community and the larger world—was a place where reporting stories was the raison d'être. Certainly, factualness in the stories was essential. But in what they do while performing their jobs, reporters are only a quaver away from fiction artists. Many of the same questions writers of fiction ask of their narrative are asked by reporters, with the primary difference being reporters' fidelity to what happened. The respect—even reverence—that writers of fiction and writers of fact have for words may explain how the zealous devotion to the spirit, if not always the hard particulars, of the *Star* style sheet must have evolved. (See page 13 for the guide's origin story).

It is impossible to look at the "good grammar" developed by the *Star* staff of the 1910s and not see solid proof that the axioms of a modern, descriptive-based grammar are how the discipline should be framed. Those intrigued by how Hemingway's style came to be should look closely at the advice that would have affected him in both the short- and long-term—and which pieces of advice he knew he would have to doctor or jettison if he were to accomplish his own goals.

Below are those rules and applications of rules that either relate to Hemingway's stylistic development or to some significant issue of grammar—or oddity therein.

Rule Number

#3 — Slang, used here, seems to denote what today would be called colloquial speech; slang here is acceptable in standard written English as "casual speech"; the caution is to avoid using clichés like "sit up and take notice" and "put one over."

#5 — Disputatious claim here: all four of the verb forms have a usefulness today, depending on what needs to be said.

#7 — "Goods valued ..." Star's distinction here is not clear; two ways of saying the same thing.

#8 — No argument here; always best to use a specific number or amount if they are known.

#9 — More on the necessity for economical expression (Puzzling note: The final sentence reads, "He said is better than he said in the course of conversation.")

#11 — Don't split verbs. Loosely adhered to by the Edwardians/Georgians; adopted by Hemingway only during the newspaper phase of his career, and even then spottily.

#12 — "The verb precedes the time"—Often awkward today ("He sold yesterday ..."), and even awkward in Hemingway's time.

#13 — Usually modifies the word it follows closest, as in "He also went"; distinguish from "He went also."

#14 — Be careful of the word "only." "He only had $10." is not the same as "He had only $10."

#17 — A useful distinction between "came" and "went."

#18 — Archaic distinction between "find" and "locate."

#19 — Useful distinction between "in" and "during."

#20 — The long-running debate between splitting infinitives or not; the "do-it" contingent has won out in our time.

#21 — Good advice about using (or not using)—ever—over-the-top adjectives like "great," "grand," and "gorgeous."

#25 — "A burglar enters a building where persons are sleeping." Use "thief" or "robber" in other cases. (No suggestions for labelling "persons" entering the building with the intention of murdering or raping.)

#26 — "Use revolver or pistol, not gun, unless a shotgun is meant." (How relatively innocent the period seems without the presence, apparently, of automatic handguns or machine guns.)

#27 — "The thief seized her purse, not grabbed or snatched."

#31 — The distinction between "should" and "would" made.

#32 — Guide sheet humor: "Don't say, 'he had his leg cut off in an accident.'" Under any circumstances, it's not likely that he'd have ordered it done.

#33 — More humor: Don't say, "He broke his leg in a fall." Say, "He suffered a broken leg in a fall." And say, "a leg," not "his leg" because he has two legs.

#39 — "Mr. Roosevelt is a leader who, we believe, would succeed." Not "whom." A grammar issue: "Who" is in the nominative case as the subject of the verb phrase "would succeed."

#41 — "None saw him except me." Caution given to not use "but" as a preposition. (As the meanings of "except" and "but" have moved closer together, this rule is absolute.)

#42 — A good reminder of the either-or, neither-nor pairing, which is still applicable.

#44 — "Say 'Chinese' not 'Chinaman.'" (A window into the culture back then.)

#45 — On euphemistic phrasing: "Bodies are not 'shipped' or 'sent'; say, the burial will be in ...." (A wartime protocol, no doubt.)

#49 — "He threw the rock," not "He threw the stone." Rock is unquarried stone. (Not a fact that too many people today would know. But Hemingway likely would have.)

#51 — Numbers less than 100 should be spelled out. (Applicable in Hemingway's time.)

#52 — "In writing about animals, use the neuter gender except when you are writing about a pet that has a name. There is it possible to use the masculine or feminine."

#54 — "The man was sentenced to be hanged" not "to be hung."

#55 — "The death sentence was executed" not "The man was executed." (This rule appears without any apology about punning).

#59 — "He was 'eager' to go not 'anxious' to go." You are anxious about a friend who is ill. (Another example of the changing meaning of words.)

#60 — All that is here to cover the use of the subjunctive is: "If I were King" not "If I was King."

#68 — Never say "the deceased."

#69 — "Such words as 'tots,' 'urchins,' 'mites of humanity' are not to be used when writing about children."

#75 — More dictional choices: "He died of heart disease, not heart failure—everyone dies of heart failure."

#79 — Don't confuse the words "habit" and "custom."

#81 — The Star does not use "dope" or "dope fiend." Use habit-forming drugs, or narcotics and addicts.

#83 — Do not use picnic as a verb. (Shall we not, then, picnic in any case?)

#84 — Portion in almost all cases refers to food. "Portion of an estate" is correct, however. (No explanation supplied).

#94 — Avoid using that too frequently but govern use largely by euphony, and strive for smoothness. (Hemingway did not talk or write very frequently about music, but it is evident that he had a euphonic sense regarding the music of his words and the rhythms of his language. The more "muscular" paragraphs of his discourse equate with percussion, but there also are musical proclamations akin to the brass instruments, and the rhapsodic swells associated with strings—violas and cellos especially. Regarding types of music, a story like "Hills Like White Elephants" is a symphonic dance, "The Snows of Kilimanjaro" a sonata, "My Old Man" an opera, *The Sun Also Rises* an Andalusian seguidilla, "Mr. and Mrs. Eliot" a fugue, and "Big Two-Hearted River" a tone poem.)

#97 — "Say a crippled boy" but not "a cripple."

#103 — Both simplicity and good taste suggest home rather than residence, and lives rather than resides.

#109 — Motor Car is preferred, but automobile is not incorrect.

The compilers clearly believed that a general directive and a few examples were enough to motivate the reporting staff to always err on the side of restraint and directness in grammatical matters—except when they didn't, or when one exceptional staff reporter decided it was time to move on.

In one of Hemingway's final *Star* articles, "Mix War, Art, and Dancing" (April 21, 1918), Hemingway was clearly stretching his imagination—and perhaps trying the patience of his editor.

Three men from Funston were wandering arm in arm along the wall looking at the exhibition of paintings by Kansas City artists. The piano player stopped. The dancers clapped and cheered and he swung into "There's a Long, Long Trail A-Winding." An infantry corporal, dancing with a swift moving girl in a red dress, bent his head close to hers and confided something about a girl in Chautauqua, Kas. In the corridor a group of girls surrounded a tow-headed young artilleryman and applauded his imitation of his pal Bill challenging the colonel, who had forgotten the password. The music stopped again and the solemn pianist rose from his stool and walked out into the hall for a drink.

This short narrative (see page 114 for complete article) begs several questions about form. Abruptly, the non-participatory narrator drops us in on an active scene: soldiers from Fort Funston (a division of Fort Riley in Manhattan, Kansas) are walking and viewing displayed artwork. Is the exhibit on a wall outdoors? Nothing indicates indoors or outdoors until the reference to "corridor," itself not easy to visualize. "There's A Long, Long Trail A-Winding" is not a musical piece that "swings"; composed in 1915 by Alonzo Elliot as a tribute to the American doughboys on their way to serve overseas, it was performed at a march tempo. Is the corporal dancing with a "swift" girl who is also a "moving" figure? Or did the author mean that she was a swift-moving girl where the adjective (participle) is modified by the now-adverb "swift"? "Red dress" as a descriptor is far too meager. With all the noise—piano, girls making a commotion around an artilleryman, and dancers—is it credible that the narrator can hear "something about a girl in Chautauqua, Kansas" being "confided"? These are compositional shortcomings that Hemingway will not make once his skills become seasoned; and it is quite surprising that his editor let such subjective and speculative prose take up column inches.

A crowd of men rushed up to the girl in the red dress to plead for the next dance. Outside the woman walked along the wet street lamp-lit sidewalk.

At this stage, the narrative is inadequate as the introduction to a feature story (presumably) about military personnel partying prior to being shipped overseas. But neither would it be adequate as the opening scene in a work of fiction. The introduction of the woman walking "along the wet street lamp-lit sidewalk" piques our curiosity, but goes nowhere. Hemingway inadvertently fuses together two independent clauses using just a comma: "The girl in red ... seated herself at the piano, the men and the girls gathered ..."

Hemingway's learning curve was steep and he was prescient enough to feed his appetite for adventure by asking his editor for assignments that would force him to confront tragedy and danger. In these articles, one can see Hemingway the reporter transitioning into Hemingway the fiction writer.

"At the End of the Ambulance Run"

The night ambulance attendants shuffled down the long, dark corridors at the General Hospital with an inert burden on the stretcher. They turned in at the receiving ward and lifted the unconscious man to the operating table. His hands were calloused and he was unkempt and ragged, a victim of a street brawl near the city market. No one knew who he was, but a receipt, bearing the name of George Anderson, for $10 paid on a home out in a little Nebraska town served to identify him.

The surgeon opened the swollen eyelids. The eyes were turned to the left. "A fracture on the left side of the skull," he said to the attendants who stood about the table. "Well, George, you're not going to finish paying for that home of yours."

"George" merely lifted a hand as though groping for something. Attendants hurriedly caught hold of him to keep him from rolling from the table. But he scratched his face in a tired, resigned way that seemed almost ridiculous, and placed his hand again at his side. Four hours later he died.

It was merely one of the many cases that come to the city dispensary from night to night—and from day to day for that matter; but the night shift, perhaps, has a wider range of the life and death tragedy—and even comedy, of the city. When "George" comes in on the soiled, bloody stretcher and the rags are stripped off and his naked, broken body lies on the white table in the glare of the surgeon's light, and he dangles on a little thread of life, while the physicians struggle grimly, it is all in the night's work, whether the thread snaps or whether it holds so that George can fight on and work and play.

Here comes another case. This time a small man limps in, supported by an ambulance man and a big policeman in uniform. "Yes, sir, we got a real robber this time—a real one—just look at him!" the big officer smiled. "He tried to hold up a drug store, and the clerks slipped one over on him. It was a—."

"Yes, but they was three of 'em, an' they was shootin' all at once," the prisoner explained. Since there was no use in attempting to deny the attempted robbery, he felt justified in offering an alibi for his frustrated prowess. "It looks like I oughtta got one of 'em, but then, maybe, I'll do better next time.

"Say, you'd better hurry up and get these clothes off of me, before they get all bloody. I don't want 'em spoiled." He was thoroughly defeated and dejected, and the red handkerchief he used for a mask still hung from his neck.

He rolled a cigarette, and as the attendants removed his clothes, a ball of lead rattled to the floor. "Whee! It went clear through, didn't it? Say, I'll be out before long, won't I, doc?"

"Yes—out of the hospital," the physician replied significantly.

Out on Twenty-seventh street a drug clerk—the one of the three who used the .38—has a .38 bullet dangling from his watch chain.

One night they brought in a negro who had been cut with a razor. It is not a mere joke about negroes using the razor—they really do it. The lower end of the man's heart had been cut away and there was not much hope for him.

Surgeons informed his relatives of the one chance that remained, and it was a very slim one. They took some stitches in his heart and the next day he had improved sufficiently to be seen by a police sergeant.

"It was just a friend of mine, boss," the negro replied weakly to questioning. The sergeant threatened and cajoled, but the negro would not tell who cut him. "Well, just stay there and die, then," the officer turned away exasperated.

But the negro did not die. He was out in a few weeks, and the police finally learned who his assailant was. He was found dead—his vitals opened by a razor.

"It's razor wounds in the African belt and slugging in the wet block. In Little Italy they prefer the sawed-off shotgun. We can almost tell what part of the city a man is from just by seeing how they did him up," one of the hospital attendants commented.

But it is not all violence and sudden death that comes to the attention of the emergency physicians. They attend the injuries and ills of charity patients. Here is a laborer who burned his foot one morning when he used too much kerosene in building the fire, and over there is a small boy brought in by his mother, who explains there is something the matter with his nose. An instrument is inserted into the nostril of the squirming youngster and is drawn forth. A grain of corn, just sprouted, dangles at the end of the steel.

One day an aged printer, his hand swollen from blood poisoning, came in. Lead from the type metal had entered a small scratch. The surgeon told him they would have to amputate his left thumb.

"Why, doc? You don't mean it do you? Why, that'd be worsen sawing the periscope off of a submarine! I've just gotta have that thumb. I'm an old-time swift. I could set my six galleys a day in my time—that was before the linotypes came in. Even now, they need my business, for some of the finest work is done by hand.

"And you go and take that finger away from me and–well, it'd mighty interesting to know how I'd ever hold a 'stick' in my hand again. Why, doc!—"

With face drawn, and heard bowed, he limped out the doorway. The French artist who vowed to commit suicide if he lost his right hand in battle might have understood the struggle the old man had alone in the darkness. Later that night the printer returned. He was very drunk.

"Just take the damn works, doc, take the whole damn works," he wept.

At one time a man from out in Kansas, a fairly likable and respectable sort of man to look at him, went on a little debauch when he came to Kansas City. It was just a little incident that the folks in the home town would never learn about. The ambulance brought him from a wine room, dead from a stroke of heart disease. At another time (it happens quite often) a young girl took poison. The physicians who saved her life seldom speak of the case. If she had died her story might have been told—but she has to live.

And so the work goes on. For one man it means a clean bed and prescriptions with whisky in it, possibly, and for another, it is a place in the potters' field. The skill of the surgeon is exercised just the same, no matter what the cause of the injury or the deserts of the patient.

The telephone bell is ringing again. "Yes, this the receiving ward," says the desk attendant. "No. 4 Police Station, you say? A shooting scrape? All right they'll be right over." And the big car speeds down the Cherry Street hill, the headlights boring a yellow funnel into the darkness.

"Mix War, Art, and Dancing"

Outside a woman walked along the wet street-lamp lit sidewalk through the sleet and snow.

Inside in the Fine Arts Institute on the sixth floor of the Y.W.C.A. Building, 1020 McGee Street, a merry crowd of soldiers from Camp Funston and Fort Leavenworth fox trotted and one-stepped with girls from the Fine Arts School while a sober faced young man pounded out the latest jazz music as he watched the moving figures. In a corner a private in the signal corps was discussing Whistler with a black haired girl who heartily agreed with him. The private had been a member of the art colony at Chicago before the war was declared.

Three men from Funston were wandering arm in arm along the wall looking at the exhibition of paintings by Kansas City artists. The piano player stopped. The dancers clapped and cheered and he swung into "There's A Long, Long Trail A-Winding." An infantry corporal, dancing with a swift moving girl in a red dress, bent his head close to hers and confided something about a girl in Chautauqua, Kas. In the corridor a group of girls surrounded a tow-headed young artilleryman and applauded his imitation of his pal Bill challenging the colonel, who had forgotten the password. The music stopped again and the solemn pianist rose from his stool and walked out into the hall for a drink.

A crowd of men rushed up to the girl in the red dress to plead for the next dance. Outside the woman walked along the wet lamp lit sidewalk.

It was the first dance for soldiers to be given under the auspices of the War Camp Community Service. Forty girls of the art school, chaperoned by Miss Winifred Sexton, secretary of the school and Mrs. J. F. Binnie were the hostesses. The idea was formulated by J. P. Robertson of the War Camp Community Service, and announcements were sent to the commandants at Camp Funston and Fort Leavenworth inviting all soldiers on leave. Posters made by the girl students were put up at Leavenworth on the interurban trains.

The first dance will be followed by others at various clubs and schools throughout the city according to Mr. Robertson.

The pianist took his seat again and the soldiers made a dash for partners. In the intermission the soldiers drank to the girls in fruit punch. The girl in red, surrounded by a crowd of men in olive drab, seated herself at the piano, the men and the girls gathered around and sang until midnight. The elevator had stopped running and so the jolly crowd bunched down the six flights of stairs and rushed waiting motor cars. After the last car had gone, the woman walked along the wet sidewalk through the sleet and looked up at the dark windows of the sixth floor.

Rule #6

Never use
old slang.

Chapter Six

Winged Lions and Seeing-Eye Dogs: Using Figurative Speech

When stuck and unable to breach the barricade that lay between the author and the action that would advance his story, young Hemingway knew the routine. It was his fallback, the precept that worked every time: the "one true sentence." No matter the severity of the blockage, all he had to do was sit back and remember a single sentence that he knew or "had seen or heard someone say." "True" seemed to mean a sentence scrupulously free from "scrollwork or ornamentation."

For many prose writers, the discipline of writing poetry—or even reading it—is therapy enough to reinvigorate the flow of prose. Hemingway was in direct touch with the poetry and poets that complemented his prose style. The mantra of Image or Imagist poetry (supplied by William Carlos Williams) was "No ideas but in things," which was not to suggest that ideas were not to be addressed by poets (or writers of fiction). Rather, abstract topics and generalized conclusions were best approached by observing and assessing how real people, real situations, and real objects operate in the world, opening the possibility of extracting general themes (the *What can it mean?*) about real-world phenomena. If he hadn't yet read

Wallace Stevens, Hemingway would nevertheless have immediately understood Stevens's thought that "Perhaps the truth depends on a walk around the lake." When Williams wrote, "So much/depends/ upon a red wheel/barrow/glazed with rain/water/beside the white/ chickens," on one level he intended his words to be taken literally: without items, objects, places, flora, fauna, machines, people—in other words, everything that takes up space in the physical world—the poet or the philosopher has no generalizations to make, thus no wisdom to pass on. That Imagist focus in Hemingway presents itself first as a love of language, second as a love of the particulars of the natural world, and, finally, with regard to what his love of the natural world signifies, as an intense love of life and living. It is there in his early writings and it remains until the sad final chapter of his life.

Hemingway's faithfulness to the *Star*'s catalogue of warnings about verbosity effectively dovetails with the beliefs and practices of the Imagist school of poetry. The height of Hemingway's production as a writer—the 1920s and '30s—coincided with the flourishing of Imagist poetry. What, if any, impact Imagism had on Hemingway, and to what extent Hemingway's compact prose exerted an influence on the Imagist poets, remains for scholarship to determine. But a common concern for simplicity and directness of speech is sufficient to open a dialogue between the two.

Hemingway attempted to write poetry—call it "pre-Imagist" poetry—composing tight, short-lined rhyming stanzas that prove poetry attracted him. But ultimately, it is possible that he never escaped the impression of his youth—that poetry, to be any good, required embellishment and overstatement. It was therefore always suspect. The *Star* style guide encouraged him to eschew any writing that employed verbal excess to distort reality. The poems he would have encountered in high school tended, typically, to be longer than one stanza. Victorian and Romantic English poets such as Matthew Arnold, Browning, Tennyson, Byron, A. C. Swinburne, and John Keats composed lines that frequently and appropriately soared, stanza after stanza, into rhapsodic realms that, even to impressionable students like young Ernest, must have seemed beyond what was necessary.

Hemingway respected poetry, occasionally wrote poems, and incorporated some poetic devices into his prose. Perhaps he came to believe that writing poetry—though not in the ornate manner of Edith Sitwell, Swinburne, or Rupert Brooke—might help him through periods of writer's block. There is no evidence that it did, but there is clear irony in the existence of many, many passages in his stories and novels being lyrical enough to be detached from their narrative, reformed, and displayed as stand-alone poems. Nevertheless, his poems were not, of themselves, of a quality that would have given him a place among the noteworthy poets of his time. To be considered a "good" poem, the language used should be fresh, and the means of transmitting the message fresh as well. But to make a poem "difficult" simply to cause a reader to wrestle with meaning is to give the poem an "un-poetic" purpose, turning it into a taunt instead of a window into human existence.

Found in Hemingway's first published collection, "Along with Youth," with its concrete references, should be a poem with a clear enough meaning for a reader to get ahold of a central message. But it is a difficult poem, and, unfortunately, intended to be so. In viable poetry, readers should be engaged in evidence gathering, not guesswork. Discourse in any genre can be cryptic, but there must be potential for the cryptic to be deciphered. In this particular effort—especially the first few lines—the references seem to float free from any clear antecedent or consequent connection. To what does the "It" in the third line refer?

Along with Youth

A porcupine skin,
Stiff with bad tanning,
It must have ended somewhere
Stuffed horned owl
Pompous
Yellow-eyed,
Chuck-wills-widow on a biassed twig
Sooted with dust.
Piles of old magazines,
Drawers of boy's letters
And the line of love
They must have ended somewhere
Yesterday's Tribune is gone
Along with youth
And the canoe that went to pieces on the beach
The year of the big storm
When the hotel burned down
At Seney, Michigan.

What can "Chuck-wills-widow on a biassed twig" possibly mean to anyone but the writer? The sequence of images actually improves in the closing ten lines, as we sense that he is collecting items that suggest the passage of time. If anything, the theme is an unfortunate reversal of the opaque beginning, as pointing out that life passes by too quickly is far too obvious to merit lyricism.

But writing poetry—especially writing it as infrequently as Hemingway did—was an adjunct exercise in another kind of concise composing, whose tools and techniques he had little familiarity with.

It was not a proper vehicle for capturing the on-the-edge lifestyle he had anticipated himself living when he left Oak Park High.

The Hemingway who resided in Paris in the early 1920s was still not yet the successful writer of prose he had hoped to become when he was a high school senior. At Gare du Nord, after being told to bring his work to Switzerland so that editor Lincoln Steffens could read it, his wife, Hadley, lost the suitcase she had filled with finished and working manuscripts, along with the carbon copies. The only stories that remained were those that had been submitted to editors of literary journals. Of this episode he wrote to Ezra Pound on January 23, 1923: "I suppose you heard about the loss of my [sic] Juvenalia?"

Between 1920 and 1924, Hemingway filed over 150 pieces to the *Toronto Star* as a freelancer, from human interest stories to reports on postwar Europe. Even on funds that barely covered food and lodging, he managed to maintain his determination to live a vigorous and adventurous life. In 1922 he purchased ski equipment for himself and Hadley, then took a train to Chamby in the Alps where they skied, partied, and drank for several weeks. Later they vacationed in Schruns in the Austrian Alps (from Thanksgiving to Easter), the Black Forest and, back in Paris, followed prizefighting and horseracing at Enghein and Auteuil, respectively. There was no dearth of material for stories during those years and Hemingway rarely struggled with writer's block. When he quit the *Toronto Star* gig, separation from newspaper work also necessitated a rethinking of how he was going to proceed as a writer. What he determined after looking at his writing style was that, while he was not about to abandon his habit of writing with descriptive precision, it needed a touch more of the lyricism that garnered attention from leading editors and publishers, who were looking for the next James Joyce.

Eventually, those stylistic choices impressed an American publishing house sufficiently, and Hemingway received a $200 advance for his "first full-length book of short stories." What stands out about those choices is not Hemingway employing figuration, but how rigorous he was when using those figures. His elemental instinct—to observe and to report without resorting to verbal excess—continued to be the key to telling a story. What was different was that he broadened the scope of his observing; he looked for more, and he saw more. Even in the long-unpublished narrative fragments there is solid evidence that his vision was expanding and that the production of full-bodied fiction such as "Fathers and Sons," "Big Two-Hearted River," "Kilimanjaro," and "Macomber"—and ultimately *The Sun Also Rises* and *For Whom the Bell Tolls*—was imminent.

Regarding figurative embellishment, what is noteworthy is how relatively rare it is to come across any figures of speech in Hemingway's prose. Figurative speech is as natural to the English language as the iambic rhythm that dominates the cadence of the sentences we construct, both in speaking and writing. Most of the time, we are not even aware that we are using figurative speech. Many such expressions originate as a way to invigorate something we want our audience to envision, and the effect is achieved most often by comparing one object or process to another, easier-to-visualize object or process. What begins as an attempt to provide clarity frequently becomes so familiar and commonly resorted to that the basis for the comparison evaporates, causing the word employed to clarify the original phenomenon to lose its metaphorical value, and thus its richness. Take the phrase "running water." It certainly derives from someone at some distant point in lexicographical history seeing the movement of water as being akin to the rapid movement of a herd of animals over a given terrain. Perhaps the comparison began as a simile: the action of water is like the act of running. Then the need to draw an express comparison using "like" or "as" (simile) evaporated in favor of a comparison where the similarity was implied (metaphor). The next semantic step would be to eliminate the need for any type of comparison-making whatsoever. We would then appreciate what "running water" denotes without a thought of those running animals. When the basis for comparison (the initial use of a figure of speech) disappears, what is left is known as a "dead metaphor."

The dead metaphor is just one example of figurative speech becoming natural, and it is employed far more than we are aware. For example, any pause in, or insertion into, discourse is a scheme called parenthesis. Repetition of consonant sounds in close proximity to one another is a scheme called alliteration. Overstating an emotional reaction is a trope known as hyperbole. Any form of contradiction expressed—whether intentional or not—is a trope called paradox. In fact, without his being aware of it, Hemingway was already a practitioner of some of the more general figures, figures each one of us uses without being conscious that we are: irony, litotes (understatement in which an affirmative is expressed by the contrary, as in "not bad"), personification, ellipsis, apposition, repetition, and formal logic.

The fact that it is difficult to date with any precision the composition of Hemingway's stories points to their consistent quality. Still, in Paris he had a sense that his writing was moving in a mature direction. Reflecting on the lost bag of manuscripts, he said, "I still had the lyric facility of boyhood that was as perishable and as deceptive as youth was." He knew that his writing style was competent at a high level and that, however its maturation occurred, it should occur naturally. Of course, he wanted to become a better writer, largely in order to exorcise one of his many demons: Hemingway maintained a lifelong professional jealousy of, among others, Stein, Joyce, the poet Ernest Walsh, and Fitzgerald. He was constantly and publicly comparing the success of his publications with those of his peers, a disposition that cost him friendship after friendship.

Stylistically, from the earliest stories to the last, his *Star* training combined with a fertile imagination to produce stylish, insightful work that—without any need for Hemingway to boast—compared favorably with the writers mentioned above. There is little self-doubt evident in the fiction he delivered in those early and middle years. In fact, there is no definitive marker where one version of Hemingway metamorphosed into another, lesser version. While his chosen method of telling a story is constant, that method is enriched by his broadening field of observation. Note that "broadening field of observation" does not mean that he was jettisoning any part of his writing style for something new; the broadening here indicates an expansion of his capacity to "see more"—in a metaphysical sense. As a dervish in his intercontinental travels, he literally saw more of the world as he matured. But, more importantly, what were truly enriched were his insights into the people he met, insights he could fashion compelling narratives around. He was a precocious young author when he devised his Nick Adams stories, but Hemingway's later fiction is frequently a deeper, more complex consideration of the values present in those stories. It was in Hemingway's nature to want to take on more, to continue to add to his already seam-stretching store of experiences. And he did so, somehow managing to detail the immensity of the world without compromising his innate efficiency in depicting settings, characters, and plots.

Hemingway was most comfortable when able to write from direct experience. "On the Quai at Smyrna" is a "tight window" account of a very particular incident through which he intended to represent

"Try and write straight English, never using slang except in Dialogue and then only when unavoidable."

— Hemingway, from a letter to his sister Carol, October 5, 1929 a broader statement about human cruelty at an international scale, drawing on his experience in Constantinople while covering the Greco-Turkish War for the *Toronto Star*. The literary device is synecdoche (a part stands for the whole) but it is such a common narrative tool that it is not something that the reader would be inclined to notice. In an odd and difficult-to-explain choice, Hemingway's "outermost" narrator—perhaps a reporter—is being addressed by another party, the "he" of the "he said" that appears in the fifth and sixth words of the story, and two or three times throughout the remainder of the story. The voice of this character—who could be an Englishman holding an officer's commission in the Greek army—relates the atrocities of a recent event in the coastal Greek city of Smyrna (now the Turkish city of Izmir) to the actual narrator. There is no need for Hemingway to drag either the etiology of the war or even the circumstances that would have resulted in the events on the quai into the story. His strategy is to let the incidents being recounted take care of themselves as he builds to his climactic—and perfectly prepared—use of irony in the story's final line. The screaming of Greek women (an ironic contrast to the classical image of the dignified Greek choruses), many of them pregnant, many with newborns, is the first of the atrocities mentioned; then the "hosing down" of the screaming women in order to silence them; the bizarre sudden death of an elderly woman, likely caused by pure fear; the human flotsam putrefying the harbor; and the abominable measures of the retreating Greek troops who, when evacuating their positions, used large clubs to break the legs of their pack animals and then shoved the helpless creatures into the shallow harbor.

It is not clear which narrator offers the story's final thoughts, but the irony is without equivocation: "It was all a pleasant business. My word yes a most pleasant business." Even the unpunctuated last sentence works well to suggest the measured hammer blow of the narrator's conclusion.

Most of the text of "Indian Camp" (see page 61) is dialogue, and it is alternately informative and pertinent, as well as crass on occasion. It is one of Hemingway's early Nick Adams stories, but "early" never disqualifies a Hemingway story from being masterfully pieced together. The narrator is omniscient, but the preponderance of dialogue used to propel the story leaves little time for that all-knowing narrator to present the thoughts of any character. After the baby's delivery, we are told that the doctor/father "[felt] exhausted"; Nick's curiosity "had been gone for a long time"; the delivering mother "did not know what had become of the baby." Hemingway's use of climax or emphasis (both rhetorical schemes) is reserved for the very abbreviated but very powerful concluding paragraph: "In the early morning on the lake sitting in the stern of the boat with his father rowing, he felt quite sure that he would never die." Nick is not being naive, nor is he being evasive. In the camp of the Indians he has had an opportunity most boys his age never do—to come face-to-face with mortality—in the form of the baby's graphic Caesarian birth and his proximity to the baby's father, who has just slashed his own throat. By being so close to death—and thus life—Nick has lost the fear of it, knowing that he will never again have to wonder what it is like to face it.

"Fathers and Sons" is another Nick Adams story, and, again, Hemingway's need for the dimension that figuration accords a discourse is minimal. Like Emerson's "transparent eyeball" that saw into and through things, Hemingway's insights and descriptive frankness provide us all we need to know. With his reporter's sense of what constitutes thoroughness, we proceed feeling assured that anything else is window dressing.

"There are certain words which are valid and similes (bring me my dictionary) are like defective ammunition (the lowest thing I can think of at this time)."

— Hemingway, from a 1953 letter to Bernard Berenson

Some stories, understandably, are best told using a variation on the conventional storytelling method. "Indian Camp" uses a typical narrative strategy: it presents events in a linear sequence, with the first event occurring in the opening words "At the lake shore there was another rowboat drawn up"—and the second at the story's close, as Nick has his existential epiphany. "Fathers and Sons" is a noticeable departure from linear storytelling. Instead of moving from the first event to the last, the author leaps ahead or steps back in time, emphasizing each event by deploying it at the point wherein it will have the biggest impact. Technically, altering the order of events in a story is a scheme called anastrophe.

The narrative of "Fathers and Sons" seems to operate in this anastrophic mode. A third-person (omniscient) speaker is driving through a small rural town with his son. They are off on a quail-hunting trip, a similar trip to one the father (Nick Adams, we quickly learn) had gone on with his father some 20 years or so ago. In one of the few instances in the text when Hemingway uses a figure of speech to stress Nick's emotional attachment to this land, even after an apparent absence of many years, the narrator refers to Nick's assessing the surroundings as being "a part of your heart." The metaphor certainly stands out; it is honest (i.e., typical Hemingway) yet forthrightly sentimental (i.e., untypical Hemingway).

The flashback occurs in the second paragraph, when Nick is thinking about all of the guidance his father gave him. Abruptly, "he started thinking about his father." In Nick's recollection, it is the father's sharp vision that first comes to mind. Some of Nick's language on this topic borders on hyperbole. "Hooked hawk nose" is an effective metaphor. The more problematic description is "His father saw as a big-horned ram saw, or as an eagle sees, literally." The "literally" is misused; since Nick is not an animal bioscientist, his clause is to be taken as a metaphor. Nick's use of the expression also calls the veracity of his statement into question. The reader grows more dubious about the clarity of the father's vision when Hemingway allows the third-person narrator to recollect the father's awkward and unhelpful explanations of "mashing," masturbation, and bestiality.

The paradoxical recollection of his father's brilliant vision and his disturbing advice leads into a related flashback in which Nick follows a trail toward an Indian village where we are introduced to Nick's friend, Billy, and Billy's sister, Trudy, with whom Nick has been having sex. The friends are likely 13 or 14. The juxtaposition of the two flashbacks—the glimpse of Nick's father and the sequence between Nick, Billy, and Trudy—suggests a kind of homage to the format of Greek tragedy. The ingredients of tragedy are present: the son, Nick, an Oedipus-like figure in search of the unqualified love of a responsible parent; Nick's father, the antagonist who fails to fulfill the role of parent, causing grave psychological damage to Nick; and Trudy and Billy, who form the protective and supportive chorus for Nick.

The words between Nick the father and his son indicate a warm and loving relationship, but all is not ideal. The son is not only inquisitive about his grandfather, he expresses a desire to visit his gravesite. The deleterious effects of Nick's father's actions (or absence of actions) are still churning in Nick's psyche, underscoring the depth of the harm done. When the son suggests a plan whereby they can visit that gravesite, though it is far away, the father's response—"We'll have to go ... I can see we'll have to go"—implies an internal debate, the essence of which is, "I don't really want to dredge up the memory of that man, but, if I am to be a better father than my father, I'm going to have to take my son to that place and let him pay his respects."

It has been decades since writers intent on learning the craft were advised to memorize the various figures of speech. And the number of terms describing the ways language can be stretched or reformed to take on other functions has changed since the era when rhetoricians like Cicero, Demosthenes, Lysias, and Quintilian made oral address the center of advanced studies as part of what was called "The Quadrivium" (rhetoric, grammar, logic, and poetics). A master orator from that period would be familiar with and be able to incorporate into his discourse hundreds of devices for making that discourse more effective. With the exception of "retro" writing programs, no writing instruction today insists on a formal learning of the terms and applications of rhetoric—which does not mean that research into "technical English usage" would prove harmful to the developing writer. The more beneficial approach would be to look them over, understand why they are important to the formation and effectiveness of discourse, and identify examples in the prose of writers like Hemingway, in order appreciate how naturally they can be deployed.

Rule #7

Use revolver or pistol, not gun, unless a shotgun is meant.

Chapter Seven

"Toto, I've a feeling that we're not in Kansas anymore": Place in Hemingway's Fiction

Whether written or spoken, fiction may be defined as a series of invented events that are infused with a dramatic element whose tension rises throughout the narrative to the point of either positive or negative resolution. Characters of different levels of importance are placed in an environment conducive to the dramatic buildup of the tension that inheres in the plot. Hemingway's short stories and novels are what they are because of his skill at creating a palpable sense of place, setting a stage for his plots to execute themselves upon. It is his facility with setting that provides the most identifiable, and attainable, elements of his style. With his newspaper background always his point of reference, Hemingway's attitude toward creating an effective location within which plots can take hold and characters thrive is, predictably, this: do what needs to be done, keeping a firm eye on the line separating "enough" from "excess." The style guide's indoctrination of exactitude through tenets likc "Use revolver or pistol, not gun, unless a shotgun is meant" are essential to making that fine line discernible.

Often enough, a story's setting impacts both the plot and the characters who carry the plot forward. Although it is rare that vagaries of setting supersede the importance of character and plot, it does happen. In any case, Hemingway's approach does not change whether the concern is the plot, characterization, or the setting: select what is effective and know when to move on. Hemingway was one of the truly talented, a writer who had maximal control over those two options.

Writers always think hard and long about where, geographically, to set the action of their story. Hemingway would have read Katherine Ann Porter's "Noon Wine" and instantly recognized how crucial her choice of a dusty, rural southern Texas town is to the plot. The especially oppressive heat of the South Texas summer sun needs to be beating down on the story's principals, dairy farmer Thompson, longtime farm employee Helton, and bounty hunter Hatch. Without the middle-of-the-day chores that continue to be done even in the midst of Hatch's threat to take Helton back to North Dakota with him, without the introduction of a "refreshing" glass of an intoxicant, wine, into the heated conversation between Thompson and Hatch, the violence—and recrimination—that ensues would seem inappropriate. Absent the particular setting, most of the actions, all of the climate-affected thoughts, and the outcome would not seem credible. What is required is what Porter supplies: literal and figurative intoxicants which combine to make this particular place and time hazardous to reasonable thinking. The location and atmosphere in this story are not simply occasions for the writer to add texture and help the reader visualize a scene; rather, those elements are as vital to the story's purpose as characterization or plot.

And Hemingway would certainly have read Stephen Crane's story, "The Open Boat," in which the natural environment—the ocean—is not merely a backdrop for the action in the story, but a major player in the fate of the four shipwrecked sailors drifting in a boat the size of a bathtub. The threat of being capsized is unceasing. The men, hunkered down in their bobbing craft, can only watch nature at work: "the horizon narrowed and widened, and dipped and rose, and at all times its edge was jagged with waves that seemed thrust up in points like rocks." Crane speaks of the waves as being "most wrongfully and barbarously abrupt and tall." Both adverbs imply a willful maliciousness, as if the narrator is personifying nature and accusing her of being morally wayward and egregiously cruel. In fact, this is precisely where Crane wishes to take his story. Scholarship on Crane has concluded that he was a "Determinist"—someone who saw much evil in the world, evil that inhered not only in humans but, in a sense, in the natural world as well. Based on what Crane absorbed from the French naturalists, the fate of all creatures is not determined by divine Providence, and the natural world is not a complement to the essential benignity of human beings—as the Romantic poets believed. Instead, nature is a powerfully indifferent force which, as often as not, proves hostile toward humans trying to make their way through the world. In "The Open Boat," the sailors ride a windswept current that eventually brings them within sight of the North Florida shoreline. But their efforts to row toward land are undermined by a cruel wind which, after blowing them within a few hundred feet of salvation, turns and blows them parallel to the shore. Desperate, the men capsize the boat and try swimming in the frigid "indifferent, flatly indifferent" January sea. Three are successful, one is not. Their welcome to the shore lies in the "sinister hospitality of the grave." Meanwhile, the exasperating and deadly waves calmly "paced to and fro in the moonlight."

Personification is the pathetic fallacy at work, the fallacy that gives nonhuman objects human attributes—as Crane does with the forces of nature in "The Open Boat." Personification is rarely the best option when a writer is looking for an effective figure of speech to color a description. Running risks that range from sentimentality to silliness, most of the time it is unnecessary, especially if the rest of the descriptive material is effective enough to get a point across. But—and this is the case with Crane—a writer who has a political or philosophical message to communicate necessitates the use of this figure. In addition to the artistic aspirations of his story, Crane's rhetorical imperative was to make sure that his deterministic philosophy received proper weight.

Hemingway appreciated Crane's stark realism—if perhaps not his occasional descriptive excesses (Crane was also a serious poet). Especially effective are the settings for his fiction, locations that included New York City's slum tenements and "bucket-O-blood" barrooms, Civil War battlefields, and a dusty, end-of-the-line Texas town. Although Crane was dead by June 1900, his gruff but credible plots, his tough-as-nails characterizations, and his advocacy for creative writers to receive far greater latitude in representing how people really speak made him popular with Modernists like Dreiser, Dos Passos, Steinbeck, Norris, and Hemingway.

Writers have many options when it comes to presenting a *setting*. In a "by-the-numbers" story presentation, the first word picture a writer would generate would be something to do with where we are in respect to what is about to occur. As you would guess, Hemingway was not one for superfluous description, even when it came to the basics of supplying a setting. "My Old Man" immerses us directly in the story: "I guess looking at it, now, my old man was cut out for a fat guy." The son's recollection of the father features only oblique

“Never confuse movement with action.”

— Advice given to Marlene Dietrich by Hemingway

references to places ("Torino," "San Siro," "Regoli"). Though no one location dominates the first 18 paragraphs, we are certainly in a recognizable environment, that of French and Italian horseracing tracks. Joe pauses to recall a specific race "at St. Cloud" pitting Kzar, a big favorite, against a long shot, Kircubbin. What becomes obvious via the details Joe unwittingly relates is that the race is fixed and it is with some difficulty that Kzar's jockey, George, can hold his horse back to ensure his defeat. With the settings established, the rest of the narrative is primarily devoted to Joe's affection for his father, his account of racetrack life, and his discovery of the various subterfuges occurring at the racetracks, which add up to introduce Joe to the sport's underworld. Joe wants to believe that his father is above participating in the criminal activity, but the whole point of the story is that the father is hip-deep in the skullduggery. The setting may be minimal, but the first-person narration is vivid and accurate enough to clearly place the reader in the desired environment.

Kipling's ability to balance concise expression with functional elaboration impressed Hemingway throughout his life. Kipling's "contained" prose style in all matters descriptive aligned perfectly with Hemingway's inclinations as a writer. Hemingway's personal library contained 22 books by Kipling, and each of them was well trod upon. Kipling and Hemingway each had a background in newspaper reporting and, periodically, took time to pay homage to the talents of the other. Hemingway biographer Jeffrey Meyers notes that his subject "did not merely imitate the British Master, but used him as an aesthetic model and learned from Kipling—more than from any American writer—how to master the art of the short story." Meyers points to [Hemingway] cutting his work to achieve what Kipling called "economy of implication," and claims Kipling "taught Hemingway how technical description could achieve verisimilitude and enhance the meaning of his fiction," as well as how to use "laconic, conversational tone." Both writers relied heavily on foreign settings for their stories; of Hemingway's novels, only *To Have and Have Not* is set in America.

Kipling exemplifies perhaps the best prose model for Hemingway. "Laconic" and "conversational" denote discourse that is in need of no garnishment. Kipling's writing may seem ornamental, but Hemingway's recognition that Kipling was a writer capable of representing a phenomenon completely proves that it is trimmed to the essentials. Kipling—and, by extension, Hemingway—followed this paradigm faithfully: short sentences clipped of their ballast, and long sentences pared down to their core. An example of how parsimoniously descriptive Kipling can be when it comes to framing the location of a story can be found in the first line of the second paragraph of the story "The Man Who Would Be King": "The beginning of everything was in a railway train upon the road to Mhow from Ajmir." After this absolutely basic reference to place, it is pure plot that propels his narrative. Descriptions helping us visualize various scenes are presented, but every passage adheres to the "no embroidery" prescription; all is in service to the movement of the plot. The first-person narrator allows Peachey Carnehan to tell his story of deception and tribal retribution in the mountains of Afghanistan; Peachey's expansiveness is Kipling's way of giving his character a distinct feature: he is a blowhard, a flaw that has already resulted in a near-death experience in the mountains. It is in Peachey's nature to give us the minutest details limning the adventures of the men who had aspired to royalty in "Kafiristan," but the excess verbiage issuing from the mouths of both Peachey and Daniel Dravot, his partner, has fatal consequences—at least for Dravot.

The bizarre culmination of the pair's activities eliminated the need for Kipling to emphasize setting once Carnehan makes his way back to our narrator's newspaper office. The denoument—the beginning of the resolution of a plot after its climax—occurs quite early in the story's development, some months after Daniel and Peachey have left for their ill-fated adventure, and not long after the bedraggled and nearly insane Peachey is discovered by the narrator outside his office. Peachey is hardly recognizable, so damaged and terrorized has he been by the Kafiristani tribe who, finally, recognize them as frauds. The narrator begs Peachey to recount the story of the journey before descending into complete madness, and Peachey complies, relating the subterfuge he and Daniel used to become kings of the tribe, the circumstances of their flight, and the pursuit of the tribal warriors after the charlatans are uncovered. The penultimate sequence, in which the narrator listens intently to the details of Dravot's demise, is potent enough that nothing more elaborate than a dark newspaper office is needed to hold it. Dravot, still believing he could convince the tribe of his regal status, was shot, crucified between two pine trees, and beheaded. If the narrator needed proof of Daniel's fate, Peachey pulls Daniel's decapitated head out of a black horsehair bag and shows it to the narrator. Peachey's psychotic state results in him being taken away to an asylum, where he dies two days later.

Writers whose plots require that characters speak in dialect invariably run into difficulty determining how to approximate—in word choice, phrase choice, variant (including phonetic) spelling, and appropriate typeset—that dialect. Every writer of dialect from Twain, Dickens, Faulkner, and Harriet Beecher Stowe to Eudora Welty, Bret Harte, and Crane (who tried to capture the patois of the Irish immigrants inhabiting the Upper East Side of Manhattan in the 1880s) has had to find a convincing way to simulate a particular speech variant. The most common advice is to avoid saturating the speech with phonetic spelling or clichés. Rather, a well-placed misspelling or occasional word in that language (if a foreign language is being simulated) suggests the dialect desired. In a similar fashion, it doesn't take very many location-specific references—city names, ethnic surnames, ethnic foods or beverages, landmarks, hotels, art galleries, indigenous animals, sporting arenas are all effective locators—to have a reader accurately surmise where an action is taking place.

All we know about place after the first three pages of Hemingway's "The Short Happy Life of Francis Macomber" is that an omniscient narrator has "dropped us in" on lunch inside "the double green fly of the dining tent." Three people are drinking gimlets. *Where* we are is revealed incidentally, as we learn about Macomber's cowardice that morning.

The frame of "Fathers and Sons" is the interior of an automobile, from which point of view a third-person narrator notes the surroundings as he (Nick Adams) and his young son pass through the "empty, brick-paved streets" en route to their destination, which appears to be a hunting camp. The terrain provides an excuse for Nick to flash back to a setting from his past, a setting in this same part of the country, that he used to visit with his father. Descriptive fragments flicker through the recollections of his father and, later, of his Native American friends as Nick relives meaningful teenage experiences. The place where Nick does his reminiscing—the automobile—is returned to for a final dialogue with his young son before the story closes out.

Stories like "Noon Wine" and "The Open Boat" privilege setting because it serves as a virtual character in the narrative. At the other extreme would be a story that categorizes setting as either marginally

"Abstract words such as glory, honor, courage, or hallow were obscene beside the concrete names of villages, the numbers of roads, the names of rivers, the numbers of regiments."

— From A Farewell to Arms

important or not important at all. "Hills Like White Elephants" is the former, "Get a Seeing-Eyed Dog" the latter. "White Elephants" is set at a railway station in Spain, somewhere between Barcelona and Madrid. The railway line parallels the Ebro River, and in the distance are the "long and white" hills. A curtain of beads across the door to the station "[keeps] out the flies." An American male is in the tableau, as is the girl he is with. Everything mentioned here constitutes the setting—and it is all packed into the first six sentences of the story. But these slender particulars are an adequate base for the heady dialogue about to take place, creating an atmosphere that suits the subject the man and the girl will be discussing: abortion. With a theme this weighty, emphasizing anything else in the discourse would provide an unwanted and unhelpful distraction.

Place in "Get a Seeing-Eyed Dog" is even sketchier than it is in "Hills Like White Elephants." Two people, a husband and wife, we assume, are trying to come to terms with the man's blindness. They are in a dwelling that has a staircase, but we don't know if it is an apartment or a house. Brief references to two towns, Torcello and Burano, suggest that the setting could be in Italy. It is raining and very windy outside, and they have a fire going in the fireplace. Hemingway has serious thematic business to deal with to try and delineate the strained relationship between the blind man, Philip, and the woman. Fixing the couple in a particular place is of very little importance given Philip's critically depressed state and his consternation about what to do with his partner. She seems genuinely concerned for the newly blind Philip and willing to take care of him, although she also says, "You know how worthless a nurse I am. I wasn't trained for it and I haven't any talent"—not exactly a sentiment Philip wants to hear. The rainy season seems to exacerbate the tension: "Do you think it will ever be spring?" he asks at one point. Philip, wanting to avoid any relationship that involves him being pitied, makes an unconvincing attempt to persuade the woman to spend some time in Paris and London so that, when she returned to him, their love for one another would be more intense. But, while struggling over whether he can feel better by "[getting] her away" and not making her his "seeing-eye" person for the rest of their lives, Philip cannot escape the consuming negativity of his thoughts. "But what else can you do? Nothing, he thought. But maybe, as you go along, you will get good at it." Holding onto the banister, a final image of his dependence, he thinks, "I must get her away and get her away as soon as I can without hurting her." In a sense, the story occurring in no particular place suggests that this hopeless situation could happen to anyone, anywhere.

It might surprise some readers that Hemingway published fables. But these fables carried, beneath the exaggerations necessary to the form, the same muscular imagery as his regular fiction, as well as sobering messages about the human condition. "The Good Lion" and "The Faithful Bull" are two such fables. Because children are commonly a significant segment of the readership of fables, setting is not an important part of the presentation. Fiction that begins "Once upon a time" is not likely to require a strict representation of place from which to launch its narrative. Africa is the setting for "The Good Lion," a land where one lion existed among others who were "bad" because they ate "zebras and wildebeests ... every kind of antelope ... and, sometimes ... people too." The good lion has wings on his back and "eats only pasta and scampi," which draws the ridicule of the bad lions. The allegorical implications become clear as the bad lions (and lionesses) squabble with—and even try to kill—the good lion. The bad lions, of course, are Hemingway's jealous peers and his many critics. The winged lion escapes their threats, speaks to them in Spanish and French, then flies off to the Piazza San Marco in Venice where he meets with his father, then heads to "Cipriani's Harry's Bar" (an actual place, frequented by Hemingway; Cipriani was the bar's owner). The good lion, however, "was changed ... from being in Africa." He adopts some of the bad habits the bad lions exhibited, but, even so, "knew that he was back home."

"The Faithful Bull" begins with a denial: he is, he says, not *the* Ferdinand (a 1936 children's book) who would rather smell flowers than fight other bulls. This bull "was always ready to fight and his coat was black and shining and his eyes were clear." The "setting" is a floating, nonspecific backdrop—aside from the fact that we are in bull-fighting country—to frame the bull's activities. The allegory is again self-referential: Hemingway-as-bull loves the fight, will take on any bull, anywhere—all a thinly veiled reflection of the kind of person he wanted to see himself as being. His desire to fight has nothing to do with anger; in accordance with "the Hemingway hero" so frequently written about in Hemingway-centered scholarship, his desire to take on all comers arises from strong self-confidence and a cool competitive spirit—he is interested simply in being the best. "Fighting was his obligation and his duty and his joy." The scene moves from various fields where he fights other bulls to a single field where his owner wants to use him to sire progeny. But the bull falls in love, refuses to "be unfaithful" to his chosen mate, and is finally sent into the bull ring, where he is tested by various matadors and killed. Hemingway was not at all known for his modesty; the allegory serves to compliment the author's vaunted strength, bravery, persistence, and ability and loyalty as a lover. One matador says, "perhaps we all should be faithful," as the bull was faithful to his mate. Yes, except that that faithfulness ensured his death.

The Sun Also Rises relies heavily on setting. The Cohn chapters lend Jake's description and assessment of this antagonistic character a fluid background. In a sweeping personal history, Cohn is depicted as a boxer at Princeton, in New York City with his wealthy Jewish family, as a man with a failed marriage, as a hanger-on in a California literary circle, as a new novelist, and, as a consequence of the arrogance stemming from the publication of his novel, as a "not so nice" person in Paris. But setting in the wake of the Cohn-centered chapters denotes a virtual tour through the restaurants, cafes, bookstores, and patisseries that depict 1920s Paris. Why anyone would want to leave this Paris is the question constantly lurking in the background as the characters move away from their hopeful, relatively peaceful home. The next two settings—Pamplona, where the Fiesta de San Fermin abruptly ignites—and the environs of the Irati River in the Pyrenees are opposites in the ambiance they present. Pamplona is a colossal debauch, at least as it is experienced by the novel's principals. Bill and Jake's excursion into the Spanish mountains has the opposite effect, revitalizing their friendship, refreshing their spirits, and offering both an opportunity to choose healthier life paths. But this cleansing is in fact an emptying out. They return to Pamplona and, once reconnected with Brett, Michael, and Cohn, the perspective picked up in the mountains proves to be powerless against the hedonism of the fiesta. Even Jake, who is putatively the most principled of the group, finds himself pimping for Brett with the bullfighter, Pedro Romero, and lying to Montoya, his old and admired friend.

San Sebastian, where Jake goes when the festival ends, is another setting that has "the power of place" in the novel. When Jake swims in the bay, it seems as though he is angling for a second chance at purification, trying to wash away all the corruption of the Pamplona experience. Since Hemingway's abiding thesis seems to be that this Lost Generation cannot escape the whirlpool of ennui that draws them in and under, the telegram from Brett begging Jake to "rescue" her once again, to come to Madrid and take her back to Paris, signals that the clarity available in San Sebastian is not something Jake can remain in; he must return to his constantly churning reality, the turmoil represented by Brett. The sunset-and-sunrise motif is circular ... and repetitive.

Hemingway, like any good writer, knew that a given story form can't be repeated too often if he was to give an audience the structural variety it subconsciously needs to continue following a particular writer. As such, Hemingway found himself having to call up some of the very pragmatic advice of his news reporter's days: **Who**? This is always central; **What**? Important, but some things will be disclosed later on for the purpose of suspense; **Where**? There is a great degree of variance about the centrality of this, but, as this chapter shows, something about place is required to "ground our perspective"; **When**? A basic time of day and a palpable duration are crucial in much of Hemingway's work; **Why**? In fiction, since the why might be what transports us from first page to last, it can be withheld.

Rule #8

Don't say "He had his leg cut off in an accident." He wouldn't have had it done for anything.

Chapter Eight

Tinker to Evers to Chance: Character and Characterization

"Character is plot." The phrase is most frequently attributed to Gustave Flaubert, but a number of writers have claimed authorship over the years. The intent of the claim is to inform writers that they needn't look any further than the lives and circumstances of their protagonists when constructing a vehicle that can transport their narrative. It is certainly not the only formula for generating a plot, but, if one thinks about how mesmerizing Flaubert's story of Emma Bovary was, the strategy is certainly a reliable one. Formula is probably too inexact a term to describe character-centered composition, since there are so many ways of blending characters and plot. But there is little doubt that an exceptionally high-impact figure is generally required to carry a plot through to conclusion. Plot builds, like coral, gradually, as the central figure's personality and actions increase the tension.

The process is organic: the more out of step a personality is with the situation into which she is thrust, the more opportunity there is for plot. In her determination to enter aristocratic society by any means possible, Emma Bovary makes decisions that, one after the other, sabotage her aspirations. Her "escape" from husband Charles consists of cuckolding him first with the wealthy womanizer, Rodolpho, then later with Leon. Her gruesome death—she poisons herself—is the inevitable end to her hopes of transcending her place in the world. Flaubert's characterization of the bright and ambitious but misguided Emma commands our attention; her behavior drives the plot even as it culminates in her suicide—a tragedy that has repercussions for Charles, who dies of a broken heart, and their daughter, Berthe, who is forced to labor in a mill.

Hemingway's cast of characters—from the heroic to the craven—was (he tells us explicitly) always based on people he knew, reconfigured enough so as to preclude lawsuits for libel or slander. The compliment he enjoyed hearing most was that he was a realistic writer. Here, then, we see one of the most important lessons picked up during his time writing for newspapers. Reporting from crime scenes and emergency rooms in Kansas City and covering wars in places like Macedonia and Spain forced Hemingway to examine and document events as they happened, and to channel them through typewriters with keys that seemed programmed to click off nothing but the truth. As outdated and overly specific as the *Star*'s style guide seems today, the rigor and attention to detail clearly fused with Hemingway's writerly core alongside the obvious dicta regarding concision. As a result, presenting characters who came across as true to life—no matter how corrupt the morals of the lowest of the low were—was a consistent goal. In a letter to his father, he wrote,

"You see I'm trying in all my stories to get the feeling of actual life across—not to just depict life—or criticize it—but to actually make it alive. So that when you have read something by me you actually experience the thing. You can't do this without putting in the bad and the ugly as well as what is beautiful. Because if it is all beautiful you can't believe in it. Things aren't that way. It is only by showing both sides—three dimensions and if possible four that you can write the way I want to."

It might be interesting for aspiring writers to know that, in his efforts to compose fiction that was realistic, Hemingway labored to "get it just right." In *A Moveable Feast*, he notes that he had started to "break down all [his] writing and get rid of all facility and try to make instead of describe ... But it was very difficult, and [he] did not know how [he] would ever write anything as long as a novel. It often took [him] a full morning of work to write a paragraph."

It is appropriate to begin an analysis of Hemingway's characterization with the type he admired most, the type that stood up to adversity with a certain kind of grace: the "Hemingway hero." In a significant number of his novels, stories, and essays, Hemingway describes behaviors—sometimes physical, but not necessarily—drawn from a variety of people from all walks of life, behaviors that rise well above the norm. Heroism of this degree within the Hemingway canon might best be embodied by Santiago from *The Old Man and the Sea*. From the beginning, Santiago is described sympathetically: a poor, old, Cuban fisherman who has a young friend who has been barred from fishing with the old man because the villagers believe Santiago is bad luck. It has been more than a month since the old man caught a fish. All Santiago seems to have left is that friendship with the boy (who reciprocates), dreams of his own boyhood in Africa, and increasingly dim hopes of catching a fish.

Yet, when tested—even at his advanced age—Santiago's determination matches that of the most elevated figures in literature. Much has been written about Santiago as a Christ figure, as someone whose response to the world's misfortune and evil is love and generosity. During his ordeal with the marlin, Santiago, tested to the limits of human endurance, performs not only courageously but with respect for the fish he is bent on killing. At some point, exhausted, Santiago manages a not-very-restful sleep; the dreams that Hemingway uses to reveal his hero's elemental self are not "of storms, nor of women, nor of great occurrences, nor of great fish, nor fights, nor contests of strengths, nor of his wife. He only dreamed of places now and of the lions on the beach. They played like young cats in the dusk and he loved them as he loved the boy." His "religion" is not the conventional Catholicism of the Caribbean—although the only rituals he can muster in his time of crisis are thought of in terms that are deeply important to that faith: sin, prayer, absolution, forgiveness, and redemption. Santiago does not have to be a zealot to be compared to Christ. Santiago concludes, "Do not think about sin. It is much too late for that and there are people who are paid to do it. Let them think about it. You were born to be a fisherman as the fish was born to be a fish." Santiago is as much about doing the work he was destined to do as Christ was about fulfilling his mission on Earth. The two share in the success of their individual endeavors: a death that is life-giving in the one instance, and a failure that is truly a triumph in the other.

Characters in Hemingway's fiction live hard and die without any special distinction. For those characters he sets aside for special recognition, one can sense Hemingway projecting himself into each of those destinies. A man with boundless energy, he was rarely without some kind of challenge, physical or literary, standing in his path. But falling short of a goal was not a disqualifier for the author of these stories; everything depended on how the confrontation was managed.

Without complaining, Santiago resolves to hold onto the marlin even if means that he will die trying. Death is at stake for the big fish as well. Santiago says, "He must pull until he dies." But Santiago's hope to kill the marlin is not thought of in terms of anger or bloodthirstiness. "I have killed this fish which is my brother," he says when the struggle is over, and compliments the fish on the courageousness of his fight. When a shark bites into the fish strapped to the side of the boat, Santiago thinks, "it was as though he himself were hit." In Hemingway's broad application of the term hero, the fish is no less heroic than Santiago.

Jake Barnes narrates *The Sun Also Rises* and is also arbiter of who gets admitted into the circle of heroes and who does not. At several junctures in the narration we find Jake observing a behavior that seems related to the standards of the circle. Brett speaks about people as being either "one of us" or "not one of us." Even with regard to characters who have "walk-on" roles, we frequently can interpret Jake's attitude toward them and determine whether they belong. Harris, whom Jake and Bill meet on their fishing trip into the mountains, is a "can't miss" candidate. Count Mippipopolous, because of his easy-going nature, generosity, and the war wounds he displays freely, is "in." Montoya, longtime friend of Jake and owner of a hotel in Pamplona, is highly esteemed by Jake for his integrity, and is *simpatico* with Jake on bullfighting. He is in the circle. Georgette Hobin, the prostitute whom Jake dines with at the beginning of the book, is not within the circle. Pedro Romero is young and has an impetuous side that puts him in the dangerous company of Lady Brett, but Romero, as a bullfighter, is the only character who lays his life on the line every day. On the second day of the fiesta at the stadium, Romero "was the whole show," according to Jake. Romero is brilliant at patiently taunting the bulls, then allowing their razor-sharp horns to pass millimeters from his abdomen:

Romero's bull-fighting gave real emotion, because he kept the absolute purity of line in his movements and always quietly and calmly let the horns pass him close each time. He did not have to emphasize their closeness ...

Romero had the old thing, the holding of his purity of line through the maximum of exposure, while he dominated the bull by making him realize he was unattainable, while he prepared him for the killing.

Romero's courage and control in the ring is a metaphor for how people ought to conduct themselves in any situation in which they find themselves facing danger—from imminent physical harm to an emotional crisis. Jake, and Hemingway, insist that a cool head is essential.

Jake is ex officio within the circle. In this postwar time he is burdened by having to live with his physical war wound and the sexual impotence that is its consequence. His depression sometimes sends him precariously close to the edge of "proper" circle behavior. Several inner circle members also do things that would seem to jeopardize their membership. Jake deceives Montoya about Romero's relationship with Brett. Brett nearly ruins Romero's bullfighting career by getting him drunk and running off to Madrid with him despite being engaged to marry Mike Campbell. Jake can't bring himself to condemn Brett for this behavior. Brett is a free spirit, a rule breaker, and an adventurer. She is also a romantic and makes decisions that are strongly influenced by her in-the-moment emotions. But she is not constitutionally flawed like Cohn. She fights fairly and is true to her friends and principles, controversial as those principles sometimes are.

The figures in *The Sun Also Rises*—Cohn included—are fascinating, regardless of our perception of them as benign or malignant personages. In fact, the characters who come across as unlikable generally draw more interest in the world of literature. (Think of how much more dimensional and colorful the character of Satan is than his divine adversary in Milton's *Paradise Lost.*) Cohn might be

"You see I'm trying in all my stories to get the feeling of actual life across—not to just depict life—or criticize it—but to actually make it alive. So that when you have read something by me you actually experience the thing."

— Hemingway, from a 1925 letter to his father

the negative force Jake thinks him to be, but his intriguing behavior begs for analysis. Hemingway wrote,

When writing a novel a writer should create living people; people not characters. A character is a caricature. If a writer can make people live there may be no great characters in his book, but it is possible that his book will remain as a whole; as an entity; as a novel ... People in a novel, not skillfully constructed characters, must be projected from the writer's assimilated experience, from his knowledge, from his head, from his heart and from all there is of him. If he ever has luck as well as seriousness and gets them out entire they will have more than one dimension and they will last a long time.

It must have seemed to his reading public in the 1920s, '30s, and '40s that Hemingway was infallible when it came to inventing characters who could not only carry the plot but also invited the closest scrutiny. But the types we come across in his later fiction are not always "living people." The portrait of Frederic Henry in *A Farewell to Arms* as an active member of the Italian ambulance corps is a valid one, though not quite as effective as Jake's. The battlefield scenes are in the best Hemingway mode, but the romantic interplay between Henry and Catherine Barkley, the nurse with whom he falls in love, runs antithetical to the dignity and style of the relationship portrayals in other stories and novels. Notwithstanding the fact that Catherine is pregnant, Henry's commitment to a political cause is called into question when he deserts the ambulance service. The language used to describe his relationship with Catherine violates in every respect Hemingway's *Kansas City Star* training in direct and compressed speech; it is mawkish, riddled with clichés, and too banal to square with the advice he always passed on to young writers. It would not be difficult to guess what his former colleagues at the *Star* would have thought about the inanity of the dialogue, the excessive verbiage of the descriptive passages, and the unacceptable sentimentality of the novel's closing pages (even considering the tragic deaths of both Catherine and the baby).

Another disappointment, on many levels, is the 1950 novel *Across the River and into the Trees*. Colonel Richard Cantwell, who fought on the Italian front in both World War I and World War II, returns to Venice shortly after the end of World War II, partially to reminisce about battles engaged in and friends made there, but more to reconnect with a young Italian girl he has fallen in love with. They have corresponded and professed their love for one another, but a wartime wound—which is never specified but seems to have resulted in a serious heart condition—has increased the urgency of their meeting. Cantwell has recently turned 50, while Renata is not yet 19. The dominant tone of the narrative is that of a reverie as Cantwell shoots ducks from a blind in the Venetian waterways early in the morning, visits barrooms and old bartender comrades, eats elaborate meals in the best restaurants, and prepares for his meeting with Renata. The novel is without the action sequences so typical—and so typically well-done—in Hemingway. It is not until we are in the last third of the book that wartime action is referenced—and then only as Cantwell recounts various skirmishes for Renata's benefit; as a native Venetian who is too young to have integrated the realities of war, she insists that Cantwell recapitulate his experiences. But the recapitulations seem too remote to affect the reader; and we never really understand Renata's purpose for pressing the Colonel on the details of his encounters. She says, "Please tell me about combat without being too brutal." He asks, "You wanted combat for what? I don't really know why. Who wants true combat ... but here it is."

"If a man writes clearly enough any one can see if he fakes."

— From Death in the Afternoon

Cantwell calls himself "Mr. Dante" and prepares to lead her into the circles of *The Inferno*, which "were unjust ... but he drew them."

In 1932, Hemingway's excellent study of bullfighting, *Death in the Afternoon*, addressed the subject of clarity (and its opposite) in writing fiction, advice he himself would later ignore while composing *Across the River*.

If a man writes clearly enough any one can see if he fakes. If he mystifies to avoid a straight statement, which is very different from breaking so-called rules of syntax or grammar to make an effect which can be obtained in no other way, the writer takes a longer time to be known as a fake and other writers who are afflicted by the same necessity will praise him in their own defense. True mysticism should not be confused with incompetence in writing which seeks to mystify where there is no mystery but is really only the necessity to fake to cover lack of knowledge or the inability to state clearly. Mysticism implies a mystery and there are many mysteries; but incompetence is not one of them; nor is overwritten journalism made literature by the injection of a false epic quality. Remember this too: all bad writers are in love with the epic.

Hemingway may have envisioned an epic—either as a reminiscence of war or a love story, or both—as he mapped out *Across the River*, but "straight statement" is not central to the discourse in this fiction. Nor is there the sense that we are in the middle of a mystical story. What we should be inclined to do is recognize an anomaly when we see one—a rather large anomaly, granted. Hemingway's status as one of the best writers America has produced is not altered if, among thousands of pages of superior prose, a small fraction of his work is not up to objective standards of good writing, never mind his own high standard.

Rule #9

He died of heart disease, not heart failure—everybody dies of "heart failure."

Chapter Nine

"And your point is ...?": Theme and Thesis Matter

Writing of the *Star* style guide for a newspaper is purposive writing, and Hemingway's editors would have made it known that his purpose while out on assignment was to represent the *Star*'s mission. Whatever ulterior creative motives Hemingway might have held on his way to a particular event had to be quickly suppressed in favor of what newspaper reporting was all about: getting the story, generating relevant and dispassionate copy, and placing it on the editor's desk in a timely manner. Personal revelations and flights of fanciful writing of any sort were to be eschewed in what was filed. But no such restrictions faced him on the other side of his journalism career. As a freelance writer in Paris, not only could he choose to take on topics that genuinely interested him—travel, hunting, fishing, politics, baseball, relationships—he could pass judgments on those topics without fear of rejection and ridicule from a scowling associate editor. While remaining within the confines of good rhetorical form—singularity of compositional purpose among them—there was now the exhilaration of having the freedom to create and pass on his vision of the world.

Hemingway's fiction is never without a central theme. How could it be otherwise with the discipline instilled during his time as a newspaper man, to compose prose with pertinence and purpose? Whether he starts with a theme or allows a theme to form naturally as setting, characters, and plot materialize, that singularity of purpose, understanding the importance of *unity*, guides the story's development. Even where a story seems to drift—in the long dialogue segments of "Hills Like White Elephants," for example—Hemingway might be likened to a pilot who has absolute control of his plane, monitoring every dial on his instrument panel as the craft banks for its final approach and then glides into the smoothest of landings. Moments of seemingly incongruous dialogue in "Hills" might appear to signify a writer who has lost his way and is using filler material to stall until cogency and purpose return. So it seems. Oblique references have the woman chatting about configurations of the landscape. There is certainly a palpable nervousness in the air—exacerbated by the actual heat on the train's platform. But there is coherence afoot: the story's *theme* turns out to be an awkward but necessary discussion about abortion. That theme will be the basis for any implied judgments the author might wish to build into his piece. Theme is usually not difficult to identify; it is the story's thesis—a judgment of the theme that is implied (or, less often, stated explicitly within the text) by the evidence of the story—that draws controversy and different interpretations.

Even if the central image of *The Sun Also Rises* is a circle wherein the participants of the primary action are, like Sisyphus, condemned to repeat their destructive behaviors, related subthemes roil in the background, not undermining the main theme, but augmenting it. Jake's clear disgust with the life he has been living suggests that the cycle can and will be broken. What really matters to Jake is courage under duress, the courage expressed so many times and in so many ways in Hemingway's narratives. But the Pamplona section of the novel reveals more cowardice than courage, and the list of those engaging in cowardly behavior extends to Jake, who cannot stand up to Brett. Things do seem to change, however, once the fiesta shuts down and Jake can reclaim his standards and sanity in San Sebastian. Even when Brett resurfaces in Madrid in the last scene of the novel, the change in Jake is discernible. Brett says, "Oh, Jake ... we could have had such a damned good time together." Jake's response is, "Yes ... Isn't it pretty to think so?" Jake's sarcasm suggests that he has the strength, finally, to draw boundaries regarding Brett. Hemingway's not-very-covert symbol of bulls (i.e., act gracefully and purposefully in times of stress) and steers (i.e., passive and, therefore, vulnerable to forces bent on doing them in), underscores Jake's determination to not let himself remain on the road to self-destruction.

Hemingway is frequently identified as an existential writer, strongly influenced by the philosophical trend that paralleled his literary production. While the philosophy emphasizes a Godless universe, the "lesson" that suited Hemingway's interpretation was that heroic behavior within this nihilistic environment was still possible: since our existence is circumscribed by time, and since there is nothing for us to look forward to outside this temporal bubble, it is the obligation of each individual to appreciate fully what it means to be alive—to celebrate, in fact, that reality. Hemingway was raised as a Congregationalist in a family that read the Bible and attended Sunday services. He converted to Catholicism to accommodate his second wife, Pauline Pfeiffer. His stories depict characters fascinated by the rituals and trappings of Catholicism. But the attraction stops at the superficial. Based on both his youthful experience in war and his proximity to the shifting philosophy present in Europe, Hemingway became an atheist. In *A Moveable Feast* he wrote, "All thinking men are atheists."

The middle-aged waiter in "A Clean, Well-Lighted Place" is not cowardly as he faces up to his disbelief in a God. But neither is he someone to be admired due to his "steer-like" capitulation. He is disillusioned and he is fearful: "What did he fear? It was not fear or dread. It was a nothing that he knew too well. It was all a nothing and a man was nothing too. It was only that and light was all it needed and a certain cleanness and order. Some lived in it and never felt it but he knew it all was nada y pues nada y nada y pues nada."

In contrast to the "existential failures," there are a number of "existential successes" as well. As his story closes down, Jake Barnes is starting to learn that there are measures that can be taken to avoid being drawn into the vortex of meaninglessness. By turning his attention to the wonders that fill his life—fishing the Irati with a good friend, San Sebastian, the tremendous meal he enjoys at Botin's, a good bottle of wine—Jake gains the potential to step off the dismal carousel of circularity and move forward.

Paco, the idealistic young waiter in "The Capital of the World," learns the hard way that life has its hazards. Late in the evening in a cafe in Madrid, Paco and two other waiters wait for the final patrons to finish their meal so that they can go home. The establishment is a microcosm of the sad condition of the world: alcoholic priests, second-rate matadors (one of whom is a complete coward), anarchists plotting against the government, and cynical older waiters. Paco, who comes from a "tiny village in a part of Extremadura where conditions were incredibly primitive," takes the position of apprentice waiter although his heart is set on becoming a famous matador. He is not troubled by the low caliber of the cafe's clientele; he is obsessed with

"Keep them people, people, people, and don't let them get to be symbols."

— Hemingway, from a 1932 letter to John Dos Passos

his dream to the point that, when the restaurant is finally empty, he convinces a savvy young dishwasher, Enrique, to strap two sharp carving knives to the rungs of a chair and pretend to be a charging bull. Enrique discusses the reality of fear in the sport; he once attempted to face down a bull in an amateur fight, and "couldn't keep from running." He resists Paco's simulation, knowing the inherent danger in even playing at bullfighting. Nevertheless, he agrees and makes several passes at Paco, who waves his waiter's towel at the blades in the stylish manner of a great bullfighter. Tragedy occurs when Enrique turns too abruptly on one of his charges. One of the chair's knives catches Paco in the abdomen and he bleeds to death before the doctor arrives. But Hemingway stresses the courage of the young waiter, who manages to embody the best aspects of bullfighting even though surrounded by abject failures in that pursuit.

Subplots and subthemes are endemic to good fiction, even within the limited space of a short story. The specifics that combine to produce a subtheme can be minimal. There are only a few references to the Catholic clergy or its practices in "The Capital of the World," but we are given a clear judgment regarding the institution. One of the waiters says about the failed matadors and the two "guzzling" priests in the cafe, "There are the two curses of Spain, the bulls and the priests." The other waiter remarks, "Only through the individual can you attack the class. It is necessary to kill the individual bull and the individual priest. All of them. Then there are no more." Paco does "not understand politics but it always gave him a thrill to hear the tall waiter speak of the necessity for killing the priests and the Guardia Civil." Paco would, the same as the politically active waiter, "like to be a good Catholic, a revolutionary ... at the same time being a bullfighter." When Paco is stabbed, Enrique runs off to find a doctor, leaving Paco to try to comprehend what has just happened to him.

Paco is alone, "first sitting up, then huddled over, then slumped on the floor, until it was over, feeling his life go out of him as dirty water empties from a bathtub when the plug is drawn." He tries to recite the Act of Contrition "and he remembers how it started," but he dies before he can finish it. The two dipsomaniacal priests are nowhere to be seen, having departed after drinking away the evening. Not all of the puzzle pieces are in place to formulate a direct indictment of the priests, but their failure to provide the dying youth with any solace is a small suggestion that the Church is far more susceptible to criticism than most thought during that time.

Both "The Short Happy Life of Francis Macomber" and "The Snows of Kilimanjaro" feature Hemingway considering death from different angles. Writing about—or, more exactly—speculating about actual death is not a topic a lot of writers of creative prose take on. In *The Death of Ivan Ilych*, Tolstoy hints at a "something" at the end of the dark sack or tunnel Ivan falls through as he passes from life. Sartre's play *No Exit* envisions a Hell made up of "other people," where we are locked in a room for eternity along with the three people we most despise in the world. Porter does her best to place her readers inside Granny Weatherall's diminishing consciousness as she moves closer and closer to her terminal jilting—by the Christ she has spent her life worshipping. Dickinson devoted much of her poetry to allowing her imagination to create a "first-person deceased" point of view. (Examples would be "I heard a fly buzz when I died," "Because I could not stop for Death," and "I died but was scarce adjusted in the tomb.") And Hemingway ponders the death experience when he has Harry soar over Mount Kilimanjaro toward good health and a hopeful life—an image that is possible only because Harry is already dead. Hemingway's representation of the interim between end-of-life and annihilation has an obvious logic: the scene contains the plane and pilot Harry had been waiting for, and a reference to the mystical history of the mountain. The capstone images—and Hemingway's final word on cosmic absurdity—contain the bizarre howl of the hyena (it makes a "strange, human, almost crying sound"), Harry's rudeness during his daughter's debut back in Rhode Island, Harry's inert "bulk" in the adjacent cot, and then Helen's discovery. The story closes with the plaintive wail of the hyena, the same unearthly sound that had awakened Helen.

The use of "Short" in the title of "Macomber" was a masterstroke. The story centers on Francis's redemption following his cowardice in the face of the charging lion. The particulars of the incident add up to form the most egregious *faux pas* anyone in the hunting party has ever seen. But the next day Macomber, having spent the night wrestling with the psychological consequences of his spinelessness, seems to have found a new resolve. Much to her surprise, Margot can sense the change in the husband she has just cuckolded with Wilson. An opportunity to prove that a shift in her husband has occurred comes when the hunting party happens upon a group of water buffalo. Margot threatens to leave her husband if he makes another scene, but Macomber is steadfast enough to call her bluff, saying that she doesn't have the gumption to leave him. It is an ironic reversal of the cowardice charge. Over the next couple of hours, Wilson, the safari guide, also notices the change in Macomber. When Wilson and Macomber go into the bushes to check on a buffalo they've supposedly killed, Macomber is excited but not afraid: "He felt a wild unreasonable happiness that he had never known before." Wilson's observation is, with regard to Macomber's new enthusiasm, "Damned if this isn't a strange one ... yesterday he's scared sick and today he's a ruddy fire-eater." Macomber's transformation is so complete that Hemingway supplies his character with the words of his model hero: "You know," he says, "I don't think I'd ever be afraid of anything again ... Something happened in me after we first saw the buff and started after him. Like a dam bursting. It was pure excitement." Wilson replies, "Cleans out your liver" and "Damn funny things happen to people." A newly impressed Wilson even quotes Shakespeare on the reason death should not be feared: "a man can die but once; we owe God a death and let it go which way it will, he that dies this year is quit for the next." Wilson concludes that he "liked this Macomber now."

Margot comments to her husband that it's rather late for him to have gotten brave, to which he replies, "Not for me." The duration of his bravery brings us back to the word "short" in the title. The term is used hyperbolically in that it denotes brevity to the extreme, a matter of hours. Nevertheless, the measure of Macomber's nobility ought not to be questioned. Margot assumes the shame of the coward when, from the truck, she shoots her husband at the base of his skull. She has realized that Macomber's newly acquired courage has altered the playing field, that he is now capable of following through on his intent to divorce her. Wilson confirms as much, saying, "He would have left you too."

Creative writers should keep in mind that, while an appropriate dose of setting is important in framing a work of fiction, and the insertion of a charismatic figure into that setting is usually even more vital, *something* has to happen to that character in order to draw a reader on. Otherwise, we have a "sketch," a descriptive profile of someone (or some place if the writer doesn't get beyond setting) that is a valid form of composition but lacks the grandeur and richness of a text with room for dramatic development. The "something that has to happen" factor should be the beginning of a series of events in which every action increases the tension. As a check on whether a basic plot has been effectively

"A writer can be compared to a well. There are as many kinds of wells as there are writers. The important thing is to have good water in the well, and it is better to take a regular amount out than to pump the well dry and wait for it to refill."

— Hemingway, from a 1958 Paris Review interview

implanted early on, an incident, disagreement, or mystery positioned toward the beginning of a narrative should cause the reader's eyebrows to raise, as if to signal, "I wonder what's going on here?"

The influence of Freudian psychology was strong during Hemingway's prime writing years. In fiction, the Freudian phenomenon translated into story lines about emotional crises playing out in the mind of a featured character. James Joyce was not the first to chart psychological turmoil, but so many of his stories involve dilemmas that are staged and resolved internally that the concept of "epiphany"—revelation—became a common descriptor of the manner in which his stories conclude. His classic story "Araby," for example, frames the aspirations of a young Dublin boy who is in the throes of his first romance with a girl whose first name he doesn't even know. She is "Mangan's sister," and he determines that he can please her by buying her a gift from the exotic-sounding bazaar, "Araby," happening downtown. On the day of the bazaar, his uncle comes home drunk, having forgotten his promise to give the boy money for the tram into the city. The tramcars are crowded and he gets "jostled" by the passengers. The bazaar is closing just as he arrives. At a booth where he hopes to find an appropriate gift, the female clerk is preoccupied, chatting with her boyfriend, and her begrudging interaction with the boy conveys that he is only an inconvenience. The lights in the building dim as the boy, giftless, turns and heads for the exit, frustrated in a mature way at the adult world's attempt to brand his romantic fantasy as adolescent foolishness. Joyce's closing sentence is, "I saw myself as a creature driven and derided by vanity and my eyes burned with anguish and anger."

Other writers whose epiphanic endings caught the attention of Hemingway are Chekhov, Tolstoy, de Maupassant, Fitzgerald, Thornton Wilder, Willa Cather, W. C. Williams, Porter, and James.

Hemingway's fiction is filled with action—bullfighting, prizefighting, cycling, hunting, trophy fishing, combat—but his plots typically winnow down to a single realization by a protagonist. The incremental education of Nick Adams is seen in the lessons he's extracted from experience, the sum total of which is a code to live by. Macomber's epiphany is real and vivid, if tragically abbreviated.

Harry in "The Snows of Kilimanjaro" is not a bad person. Rather, he is put in the uncomfortable position of assessing his life as it starts to ebb. The entire story is—interestingly and unusually—an extended epiphany that culminates in that final delusion, the belief that he is soaring toward a new life. The circumstances of gangrene afford him the unpleasantness of seeing himself as he was, and seeing himself in the present as he interacts with his wife. While the self-appraisal isn't catastrophic, neither is the end result satisfactory. Harry is forced to face nemeses such as irascibility, cynicism, slothfulness, womanizing, and taking advantage of his wealthy wife. And, unable to resolve these defects, he simply starts over again.

Sadder than Harry's slow and painful coming-to-terms is the lightning-fast reckoning that is forced upon Paco in "The Capital of the World." Clearly, he can barely understand what is happening to him. A half-hour prior to the tragedy he was just a boy working as a waiter, dreaming of a life as a bullfighter. His last human contacts were Enrique and the trickle of customers who finally leave the restaurant. But Paco had no chance to get to know these people or understand what their lives consisted of, how their lives might end. "He died ... full of illusions ... He had not even had time to be disappointed in the Garbo picture which disappointed all Madrid for a week."

These are the gossamer threads of human behavior and psychology that Hemingway wove, and the webs he formed captured a number of profound insights into what makes us tick. The epiphanies his characters experience strike us as plausible, and, not infrequently, applicable to ourselves, because of Hemingway's careful selection of the decisions and actions that preceded the perceptions. This ability to provide a proper foundation for these leaps of logic is a direct result of the eye for detail and nuance he developed as a reporter. Because, as Rule No. 75 points out, we all die from the same thing, but why and how is a whole other matter.

Rule #10

Use vigorous English.

Chapter Ten

Write like Hemingway: A Lineage, a Legacy, and a License

An authentic genealogical chart of writers whose prose innovations made Hemingway's style possible would require going back centuries, likely to the *Tales of the Magicians*, an Egyptian manuscript from approximately 4,000 BCE. But a more identifiable starting place would be Edgar Allan Poe in the mid-nineteenth century, as he developed a style and perspective the influences of which continue into the present. Most prose written in the mid-1800s was far wordier than it needed to be. Nevertheless, it corresponded to the attention span of its audience, who devoted a large percentage of their leisure time to reading, and to suit the aesthetic requirements created by generations that had appreciated the eloquence and elaboration of a Dickens or a Hugo, a Brontë or a Melville.

Poe not only wrote short stories, he was also a theorist who devised forms and strictures for the genre. A good deal of scholarship has traced both the Gothic and the symbolic strains of Hemingway's prose back to Poe, who gave that genre an American identity, promoted and practiced the symbolism of the French avant-gardists, composed critical essays that were among the best of his time, and wrote poetry in which the language proved as delightful as the meaning derived. Hemingway called Poe's writing "skillful" and "marvelously constructed." The writers Hemingway read and acknowledged as proximate influences—Flaubert, Tolstoy, Chekhov, and Kipling, along with Poe—were all Symbolists, albeit to different degrees.

Good writers don't "write symbolism into" their stories. That caution is so basic that it doesn't even need to be listed among the tenets of the *Kansas City Star's* style guide. No reporter would consider turning in copy garnished with animism, metaphor, simile, or any other *figure*. No, they lived by the most fundamental rule: "Use vigorous English."

Good writers of fiction concentrate on making it clear that a dramatic incident has occurred. Once that incident has been outlined, it generates a tension that must be resolved before the affected parties can move on. The goal is the "compression of a maximum of life within a minimum of space." As there are always layers of meaning beneath what we say to someone, so, too, are there subcutaneous meanings residing in the events of a narrative. But those underlying elements can never be the focus. To stay clear of this trap, one would do well to keep one of the key imperatives of the *Star* style guide in mind: keep the story as simple and as straightforward as possible, having faith that meaning will bubble up if this is accomplished.

In a letter to critic Edmund Wilson, Hemingway denies the "charge" that he was a Symbolist, discussing his focus when composing *The Old Man and the Sea*:

You know I was thinking about actual sharks when I wrote the book and had nothing to do with the theory that they represented critics. I don't know who thought that up. I have always hoped for sound, intelligent criticism all my life as writing is the loneliest of all trades.

"Write as long as you can live."

— From _Green Hills of Africa_

Hemingway's denial notwithstanding, the shark attacks on Santiago's fish have literal and figurative functions. As the ocean where the big fish first takes the lure (and perhaps precisely there) is many fathoms deep, so are the strata of meaning in this rich story. Hemingway concentrated, as all good writers should, on his story line, not on "layer building." But—again acknowledging his denial—if the surface or literal level of a narrative has been set down with accuracy and clarity, the reader can expect to find a layer of meanings awaiting examination. The search for meanings beneath the surface honors the genius of the artist whose complex work reflects how the most sophisticated of human minds work.

Hemingway scholars have invited us to think of Santiago's courage and determination as being akin to those qualities Christ displays in the Gospels. Santiago might say, "I am not religious," but he certainly enacts a Christian role in the way he, as a God-the-Father type, cares about the God-the-Son figure, Manolin. Santiago's three-day contest with the fish may be said to resemble Christ's Passion, crucifixion, and death. The image of Santiago trying to drag his boat's mast up from the shore when he does return to the harbor suggests Christ bearing the cross against which he will be nailed; his palms being torn as he tries to hold on to the fish correspond to the spikes driven into Christ's palms on the cross.

Another interpretation of this symbolic tableau views the ordeal as Hemingway reflecting on his own history as a once-successful writer now being forced to cope with his failures as he makes one last noble attempt to create high art. As Santiago has gone 84 days without a catch, so Hemingway experienced a long spell without repeating the success—and positive critical reception—of *The Sun Also Rises* and *For Whom the Bell Tolls*. The mutilation of the marlin by the sharks is a metaphor for what Hemingway perceived as the critical savaging of his literary output since those early novels. Exhausted yet heroic in his confrontation with the majestic marlin, Santiago's triumph is also Hemingway's triumph as a reconstituted novelist. And that triumph went beyond the personal—the critical reception of *The Old Man and the Sea* was so overwhelmingly positive that it prompted a complete reassessment of Hemingway's oeuvre.

When the last shark falls away with the last bit of the fish's flesh, the tone shifts dramatically, moving from frantic resolve to relief that the ordeal is over. Even though there is no trophy to display to the other fisherman and the townspeople, Santiago has the satisfaction of knowing that he has faced up to the most severe test nature could send his way, and that he will live to do what he wants most to do: share his story with his young friend Manolin. Santiago is disappointed, but, having proved himself to himself, he is also relieved:

He sailed lightly now and he had no thoughts nor any feelings of any kind. He was past everything now and he sailed the skiff to make his home port as well and as intelligently as he could. In the night sharks hit the carcass as someone might pick up crumbs from the table. The old man paid no attention to them and did not pay any attention to anything except steering. He only noticed how lightly and how well the skiff sailed now there was no great weight beside her. ... He could feel that he was inside the current now and he could see the lights of the beach colonies along the shore. He knew where he was now and it was nothing to get home.

The Old Man and the Sea, published in 1952, was Hemingway's announcement that he had returned as a writer. There is no contrast more stark than the quality of *The Old Man and the Sea* and the 1950 disaster, *Across the River and into the Trees.* In a letter to critic Robert Cantwell about *Across the River*, Hemingway wrote:

Book is truly very good. You pan it to hell if you don't like it. That is your right and your duty. But I have read it 206 times to try and make it better and to cut out any mistakes or injustices and on the last reading I loved it very much and it broke my fucking heart for the 206th time. This is only a personal reaction and should be discounted as such. But have been around quite a while reading and writing and can tell shit from the other things.

Apparently not. It was clearly not one of the "other things." Colonel Cantwell is driven through various Italian villages by an NCO chauffeur who seems as bored by the tedious reflections on past battles as the reader is. Cantwell's reunion with the very young Renata serves as the engine for the narrative, but it never really gets started. Their love is improbable—on both sides, as the reasons for Cantwell's attraction to her are never made clear. Their conversations consist of standard exchanges of endearment, reminiscent of the very ordinary—and banally melodramatic—dialogue between Catherine Barkley and Frederic Henry in *A Farewell to Arms*. Hemingway's own infatuation with a young Italian woman is often given as his impetus for writing the book, but the long flashbacks detailing fighting in the trenches and duck hunting in the cold waters of Venice's canals blunt any passion. An English translation of "Renata" is "reborn," but—so untypical of Hemingway theses—there is little that suggests renewal in this work. Even Cantwell's heart attack and death at the end doesn't provide the reader closure—since there is so very little tension that needs resolving.

The 1935 memoir *Green Hills of Africa* is one of those "other things," and, unfortunately, is frequently overlooked as being so. While the events and people are real and the narrator is Hemingway himself, the book reads like a novel. There is deep tension between several members of the safari—between Hemingway and another safari hunter, Karl, and between Hemingway and several of the African guides. There is tension between the pursued and the pursuer, the hunting party and the unpredictable game roaming the savannas. There is a very particular tension involving Hemingway's pressing need to kill a kudu, a species of antelope with large, corkscrew-shaped horns, before the safari is scheduled to end. This final tension builds to a climax reached within the final 30 pages.

The book is also a wellspring of commentaries on the craft of writing. Hemingway discusses writing sometimes in response to inquiries from companions identified as Pop and Kandisky (a European expatriate), and sometimes simply out of a need to address topics from his professional life. He writes about how it is a practice for the French parents of aspiring young writers to agree to fund those aspiring writers for a two-year period. If, at the end of the allotted time, the son has not published anything noteworthy, he is obliged to return home and enter the father's business. Hemingway disagrees with the practice. "Write as long as you can live," he says, "and there is pencil and paper or ink or any machine to do it with, or anything you care to write about, and you feel a fool, and you are a fool, to do it any other way." Kandisky quizzes him about whom he considers the best American writers. Hemingway names Emerson, Hawthorne, and Whittier, but chastises them for doing nothing new with either language or theme; "very dull" is how he concludes his assessment. Hemingway is also concerned that, among the writing community, there is too much "inter-influencing" going on:

Writers should work alone. They should see each other only after their work is done, and not too often then. Otherwise they become like writers in New York. All angleworms in a bottle, trying to derive knowledge and nourishment from their own contact and from the bottle. Sometimes the bottle is shaped art, sometimes economics, sometimes economic-religion. But once they are in the bottle they stay there. They are lonesome outside of the bottle. They do not want to be lonesome.

It is in the context of this book that Hemingway expresses his oft-cited praise for Twain's achievement with *Huckleberry Finn*: "All modern American literature comes from ... *Huckleberry Finn*. ... There was nothing before. There has been nothing as good since."

Hemingway excoriates writers who write "to keep up their establishments, their wives, and so on, and they write slop. It is slop not on purpose but because it is hurried. Because they write when there is nothing to say or no water in the well. Because they are ambitious." "Quite good" books, he says, "are panned by critics, and that criticism has, among too many writers, rendered them impotent." "Writers are ruined by first money, the first praise, the first attack, the first time they find that they cannot write, or the first time they cannot do anything else." And, in a comment that ought to be a mantra for all who want to write: "I must write because if I do not write a certain amount I do not enjoy the rest of my life."

Hemingway turns uncharacteristically mystical when asked by Kandisky about whether prose has limitations:

First, there must be talent, much talent. Talent such as Kipling had. Then there must be discipline. The discipline of Flaubert. Then there must be the conception of what it can be and an absolute conscience as unchanging as the standard meter in Paris, to prevent faking. Then the writer must be intelligent and disinterested and above all he must survive. Try to get all these in one person and have him come through all the influences that press on a writer. The hardest thing, because time is so short, is for him to survive and get his work done. But I would like us to have such a writer, and to read what he would write.

The plot of *Green Hills of Africa* moves at a pace in harmony with its subject matter, hunting wild animals. With the prospect of game close by but just out of sight, there is little time for reflection. There is a rush for the rifles and the open-top vehicles that will put the hunters within range. At times the pace slows to a deep-grass trudge in pursuit of a quarry whose trail goes completely cold. Hemingway seems always on the brink of pulling the trigger to take down a kudu bull, only to discover that the bull is actually a cow with calves nearby—and off-limits to a hunter. Within the party there is a palpable tension: Karl is an independent hunter who is bent on "cutting" Hemingway's reputation as a top-notch figure in their sport, and, although their animosity doesn't rise to the level of a physical bout, they box metaphorically by testily comparing the girth of, or hooves of, or antlers of, or horns of different types of game each has brought down. There is also an ongoing conflict between Hemingway and several of the African gun bearers and trackers whom he considers inept.

The quality of the descriptive passages throughout the novel matches the best of his early fiction:

The afternoon of the day we came into the country we walked about four miles from camp along a deep rhino trail that graded through the grassy hills with their abandoned orchard-looking trees, as smoothly and evenly as though an engineer had planned it. The trail was about a foot deep in the ground and smoothly worn and we left it where it slanted down through a divide in the hills like a dry irrigation ditch and climbed, sweating, the small, steep hill on the right to sit there with our backs against the hilltop and glass the country. It was a green, pleasant country, with hills below the forest that grew thick on the side of a mountain, and it was cut by the valleys of several water-courses that came down out of the thick timber on the mountain. Fingers of the forest came down onto the heads of some of the slopes and it was there, at the forest edge, that we watched for rhino to come out.

Lyricism of this kind is what lends texture to Jake's fishing expedition into the Pyrenees with Bill Gorton in *The Sun Also Rises*, and to a similar adventure detailed in the story "Big Two-Hearted River." No less vivid but of an entirely different type is the ability Hemingway has in *Green Hills* to describe shooting and killing water buffalo, antelope, and rhino. One particularly graphic passage describes the sound of a large-caliber bullet striking the skull of a hyena, while another details decapitating, disemboweling, and preparing a "trophy kill" for shipment back to the United States. Hemingway's exposure to Poe's descriptive frankness is evinced here, but his own experience tending to the dead and wounded on the battlefields of Italy in World War I seems an even larger influence. Hemingway thinks about "what a great advantage an experience of war was to a writer." He mentions Tolstoy as someone gravely affected by war, and Flaubert, who experienced not war but revolution. Dostoevsky's war was political, and he was sent off to Siberia; Stendhal had seen a Napoleonic war. Hemingway observed that "Writers are forged in injustice as a sword is forged."

Hemingway was a Symbolist, a Minimalist, an Imagist, and a Modernist. Outside those labels and above all, he was a naturally talented writer. Anyone interested in writing like Hemingway would have to absorb the forms and the rhythms of his syntax, and buy into the belief that the elements of a story (setting, character, plot, tension, tension-release) are best rendered with only the essentials. But what is ultimately required is the most difficult: drawing abreast of the passion that made him want to be a writer, and, second, made

"Don't get discouraged because there's a lot of mechanical work to writing. There is, and you can't get out of it. I rewrote <u>A Farewell to Arms</u> at least fifty times. You've got to work it over."

— Advice given to Arnold Samuelson by Hemingway, ca. 1934

him want to be America's premier writer. "Technical Hemingway" is accessible by reading a handful of his stories, noting what he does to bring every sentence alive, and then practicing those forms to the point that you can emulate the style of the originator. But to feel the passion that gave him the motivation to forge his original style, nothing less than a close reading of his entire output—including his correspondence—is necessary.

A collateral reading project would entail looking back over his earliest newspaper articles—articles informed by the strictures of the *Star* style guide—and reading to gain a sense of the dynamism in his sentences that, from the very beginning, signaled a clear wish to do more than simply report the news.

All of these "attachment" strategies are a form of sharing Hemingway's legacy as a writer, of directing hopeful writers into a virtual but potentially very useful seminar guided—if *in absentia*—by one of America's foremost masters of letters.

And the idea of "write like ..." can be made even more substantial if the curriculum and the exercises were extended to those writers who proved inspirational to Hemingway: Poe, Flaubert, Tolstoy, Chekhov, Kipling, et al. Read as much as you can of each author—at least until you have a feeling for style and common themes. Try to sense what it was about each author that so attracted Hemingway. There would, of course, be no possibility of failure with such an endeavor. At the very least, readers would come away from the project having spent quality time with some of humanity's best and most creative thinkers.

In 1979, Norman Mailer, who had just published *The Executioner's Song* and was at the height of his powers, offered this appraisal of Hemingway: "So I wrote the Gilmore book simply. Maybe it led me to think that I could take a crack at Hemingway, but the fact of the matter is, when it comes to writing simply, I am not Hemingway's equal. My great admiration for Hemingway is not necessarily for the man, the character. I think if we had met it could have been a small disaster for me. But he showed us, as no one else ever has, what the potential strength of the English sentence could be."

Remember, above all else: "Use vigorous English."

"On the *Star* you were forced to learn to write a simple declarative sentence. This is useful to anyone."

— Hemingway, from a 1958 Paris Review interview

Appendix

These three Kansas City Star *stories were written by Hemingway and demonstrate how the young man was growing into his talent, as well as becoming increasingly anxious to leave the country in order to witness and experience World War I in person.*

"Kerensky, The Fighting Flea"
December 16, 1917

Somehow, although he is the smallest office boy around the place, none of the other lads pick on him. Scuffling and fighting almost has ceased since Kerensky came to work. That's only one of the nicknames of Leo Kobreen, and was assigned to him because of a considerable facial resemblance to the perpetually fleeing Russian statesman, and, too, because both wore quite formal standing collars.

In size, Leo is about right for spanking. But that never will happen to Leo. Although he is inches short of five feet, there is a bulkiness about his shoulders that gains respect even from those Cossacks of the business world, the messenger boys.

In fact, it was a messenger, coming in blusteringly, who first made it known that Leo possessed a reputation. Almost politely the cocky young fellow handed a yellow envelope to the office bantam.

"Why it's Kid Williams," he said, "Are you going to fight at the club Saturday night, Kid?"

"I should have known it," the boss said, "Kerensky has all the characteristics of a prize fighter. After a short round of work doesn't he retire to a corner and sit down?"

Then some of them remembered Kid Williams in preliminary bouts ... One of those boys who scrap three rounds before the big fighters enter the ring. That's Kerensky.

You may have thrown some loose change into the ring at the final gong. How you laughed to see the two bantams push each other about and scramble fiercely each to pick up the most. Sometimes they couldn't wait to get their gloves off. All the fight fans roared at them trying to pick up thin dimes in their padded fists.

"That's all hippodrome stuff," Kerensky says. "The men like to see us quarrel over the money, but win or lose, we split it fifty-fifty. My half of the pickup runs form $1.50 to $2.50."

The worst thing about the fight game, take it from Kerensky, is the smoke. He has even considered retiring from the ring because it is so upsetting to take a deep breath of tobacco fumes.

"But of course I haven't quit," he explains. "Right now if I knew some of the clubs downtown had a smoker on and they offered me $2, of course I'd get in and fight."

How would Kerensky advise a young man to open a pugilistic career? Well, he just picked up his skill. For several years he sold papers, and you know how one thing leads to another. There is a newsboy rule that if one boy installs himself on a corner no other can sell there. A full grown man used to cry the headlines on a certain Grand Avenue crossing. Poachers bothered him.

"It wouldn't look right for a big fellow to hit a little kid," says Kerensky, "so he let me sell there, too, and sicked me on all the strange boys. I always ran them away. He liked me and called me Kid Williams, after the bantamweight champion."

Kerensky's last street fight was to a big gate. A newsboy of larger growth was the victim. They clinched and fell to the sidewalk. A crowd gathered, but the crossing patrolman turned his back till the battle was over. Then he came over and said: "Leo, I guess you'll have to cut this out."

After that, when Leo wanted to fight, somebody had to hire a hall. He began going into the gymnasiums to sell papers. There he watched the big men train for their Convention Hall bouts. Sometimes the proprietors would let him come in and work out beside Thorpe or Chavez for nothing. It costs the ordinary citizen a dime, Leo says, to get in and work at the pulleys and weights at times like these.

His opportunity came to go on in a newsboy bout at a smoker in Cutler's gymnasium. The kid glows yet at the mention of that bout.

"It was the best fight of my career," he says. "I went in mad, and gave the fans their money's worth. But I was awful green, and was almost knocked out in the last round. Now I know how to study 'em, and I don't have to work as hard."

After hard days in old Russia, the life is full of joy for Leo, and who can say that he is not making the most of his opportunities? When he talks of the past it is of a program. That Christmas season the workmen in a sugar refinery near Kiev made a cross of ice and set it up on the frozen river. It fell over and they blamed the Jews. Then the workmen rioted, breaking into stores and smashing windows. Leo and his family hid on the roof for three days, and his sister fell ill of pneumonia. One studies to change the subject and asks:

"Leo, do they ever match you with a bigger boy?"

"Oh no," he says, "the crowd wouldn't stand for that. But sometimes I catch one on the street."

"Battle of Raid Squads"
January 6, 1918

John M. Tully and Albert Raithel, revenue officers from St. Louis, may die, and two city detectives narrowly escaped injury as a result of a revolver battle yesterday through a case of mistaken identity.

Tully and Raithel had gone to raid a house at 2743 Mercier Street, reported to be a rendezvous for drug users. Edward Kritser and Paul Conrad, city detectives, arrived a few minutes later on the same mission. Each party of officers mistook the other for drug peddlers.

Tully was shot in the right leg, left arm and lower abdomen. Raithel was wounded in the abdomen and left wrist. Both will recover. The two detectives were uninjured, but both had bullet holes through their clothing.

The wounded men were taken to the General Hospital. Later they were removed to the Swedish Hospital.

While on the surface the shooting of the two government officers appeared to be a case of mistaken identity, elements of a mysterious nature which Francis M. Wilson, United States district attorney, refused to make public, crept into the case last night.

At 11 o'clock last night the district attorney took a statement from Tully. He said he could not disclose its contents. It was admitted by another government official there was "something back of the whole affair."

It was said all of the evidence with regard to the shooting and developments leading to the affair will be placed before Hunt C. Moore, prosecutor. Senator Wilson said the government would co-operate with the prosecutor. The district attorney conferred two hours last night with Chief Flahive and John Halpin, police commissioner. At the close Senator Wilson said he felt certain the prosecuting attorney would do his duty in the case.

Tully gave this story of the shooting:

"Raithel and I received information that there was a nest of drug addicts at a house at 2743 Mercier Street. We secured a search warrant from S.O. Hargis, assistant United States district attorney, and went out. In the house was an old woman. We questioned her and could learn nothing, so left to watch the house and question a few of the neighbors. We were standing across the street when a motor car drove up and two men and a girl got out. One of the men carried a handbag. Raithel and I thought they were 'dope heads.' I went to the front door and Raithel to the rear. Inside the door I saw Bernie Lamar's girl. She said, 'Hello Jack.' Then a man stepped out of the next room. I walked up to him and touched him on the shoulder, saying, 'Hold on a minute, I'm an officer.' Then he started shooting. He got me in the arm. I shot twice and then got out the door. I got across the street and fell in front of a house. Then the other man shot me again. I emptied my revolver and then staggered over to a garage across the road."

Raithel was operated on as soon as he was taken to the hospital and was unable to make a statement.

The two detectives told a different story. According to them the battle was the culmination of a feud between a gang of drug addicts and government agents.

About seven months ago Bernard Aberer, a notorious police character, was sent to the Fort Leavenworth prison for drug peddling. John Tully had secured the evidence that convicted Aberer. His wife, Rose Aberer, alias Rose Fuqua, known as Rose Lamar, has been living here with a man named William "Irish" Rogers, also a drug addict and holder of a police record. When Tully arrested Aberer the government secured a large quantity of narcotics. Lately the federal officials here have been trailing Rose Fuqua, trying to locate the rest of the big supply of drugs which she was believed to have hidden.

Two special agents were sent from the St. Louis office to aid in the work.

Friday night Rose Fuqua and Williams were shadowed to the Stratford Hotel, 616 East Eighth Street, where they registered as Mr. and Mrs. William Sullivan. Yesterday the revenue office obtained two detectives from police headquarters to aid in raiding the room at the Stratford. Kritser and Conrad were assigned. Rose, a man named Richard C. Adams, and Rogers were arrested in the room and a quantity of narcotics found. The woman confessed to the government agents that the missing drugs were hidden in her mother's home at 2743 Mercier Street. The city detectives took her and Rodgers out to the address.

Conrad and Kritzer found a sack containing a quantity of heroin, morphine, opium and two complete "hop smoking" outfits hidden in the house. Conrad says he was talking to Rose Fuqua in the front room of the 5-room frame house when he heard a knock on the door. A man entered. The woman said, "Hello, Jack, how are you?" Conrad said in a sworn statement.

"I concluded from the familiar way he spoke to her that he was a member of the gang," the detective said. "The man turned to me and said 'Who are you?' reached for his revolver and reached for my shoulder. I drew my revolver and fired twice. He shot at me three times. One bullet went through my coat, another grazed the side of my face. My shot struck him and he reeled out of the front door. Another man (Raithel) shot at me through the window. I fired three times and then went behind a door to reload my gun.

"I heard someone shooting in the rear of the house and saw Kritser shooting at a man across the street. I stepped around and exchanged shots with a man shooting from behind a grocery wagon. I thought we were fighting a gang of dope fiends and rushed to the next house on the north, firing as I went. Kritser and I both shot at a man firing across the street. The small man dropped. Someone yelled, 'They're government men.' We stopped firing. Neither one of them said anything about being officers to me."

Kritser's story and that told by Rose Fuqua agreed with Conrad's. Rose Fuqua and Rogers escaped in the fight, but later gave themselves up.

Buddie, a dog owned by Rogers, was shot in the leg and is being taken care of by a neighbor. Adams, Rogers, and Rose Fuqua are being held at police headquarters for investigation.

"Six Men Become Tankers"
April 17, 1918

Six men were accepted today for the new tank corps by Lieut. Frank E. Cooter, who arrived from Washington yesterday to recruit men for the special service. The men were selected from a crowd of twenty that appeared at the army recruiting office at Twelfth Street and Grand Avenue today. Men of various occupations, from bookkeepers to motor operators, applied for service today. Those accepted are:

Elvin L. Loyd, 1711 Penn Street, a tractor driver.

Harold E. McEachron, Atlanta, Ga., a machinist.

Kenneth C. Dills, 3939 Agnes Avenue, stenographer.

Robert E. Watson, 1317 West Thirteenth Street, stenographer.

Albert F. Henne, 207 East Twelfth Street.

Lewis M. Dean, Chicago, Ill.

The men of the tank corps enlist in a dangerous branch of the service, but it is thrilling work and, like aviation, has long periods of rest and inactivity between the short, concentrated spells of action.

All the men taken were of draft age and were given a letter from Col. I.C. Welborn of the tank corps, authorizing any local board to immediately induct them into service.

A returned officer from the western front now training recruits at the national tank training camp at Gettysburg, Pa., tells the inside story of one of the land ships in action.

For several days the men prepare for the coming offensive. The tanks are brought up behind the first line trenches under cover of darkness and the crews crawl into the close, oily smelling steel shells. The machine gunners, artillerymen and engineers get into their cramped quarters, the commander crawls into his seat, the engines clatter and pound and the great steel monster clanks lumberingly forward. The commander is the brains and the eyes of the tank. He sits crouched close under the fore turret and has a view of the jumbled terrain of the battle field through a narrow slit. The engineer is the heart of the machine, for he changes the tank from a mere protection into a living, moving fighter.

The constant noise is the big thing in a tank attack. The Germans have no difficulty seeing the big machine as it wallows forward over the mud and a constant stream of machine gun bullets plays on the armour, seeking any crevice. The machine gun bullets do no harm except to cut the camouflage paint from the sides.

The tank lurches forward, climbs up, and then slides gently down like an otter on an ice slide. The guns are roaring inside and the machine guns making a steady typewriter clatter. Inside the tank the atmosphere becomes intolerable for want of fresh air and reeks with the smell of burnt oil, gas fumes, engine exhaust and gunpowder.

The crew inside work the guns while the constant clatter of bullets on the armour sounds like rain on a tin roof. Shells are bursting close to the tank, and a direct hit rocks the monster. But the tank hesitates only a moment and lumbers on. Barb wire is crunched, trenches crossed and machine gun parapets smothered into the mud.

Then a whistle blows, the rear door of the tank is opened and the men, covered with grease, their faces black with the smoke of the guns, crowd out of the narrow opening to cheer as the brown waves of the infantry sweep past. Then its back to barracks and rest.

"We want fighters for the tank service," said Lieutenant Cooter today. "Real men that want to see action. No mollycoddles need apply." Men from 18 to 40 years old are being enlisted at the army recruiting station, Twelfth Street and Grand Avenue. Men of nearly all mechanical trades may enlist if they pass the personal inspection and mental test given by Lieutenant Cooter.

Ernest Hemingway Timeline

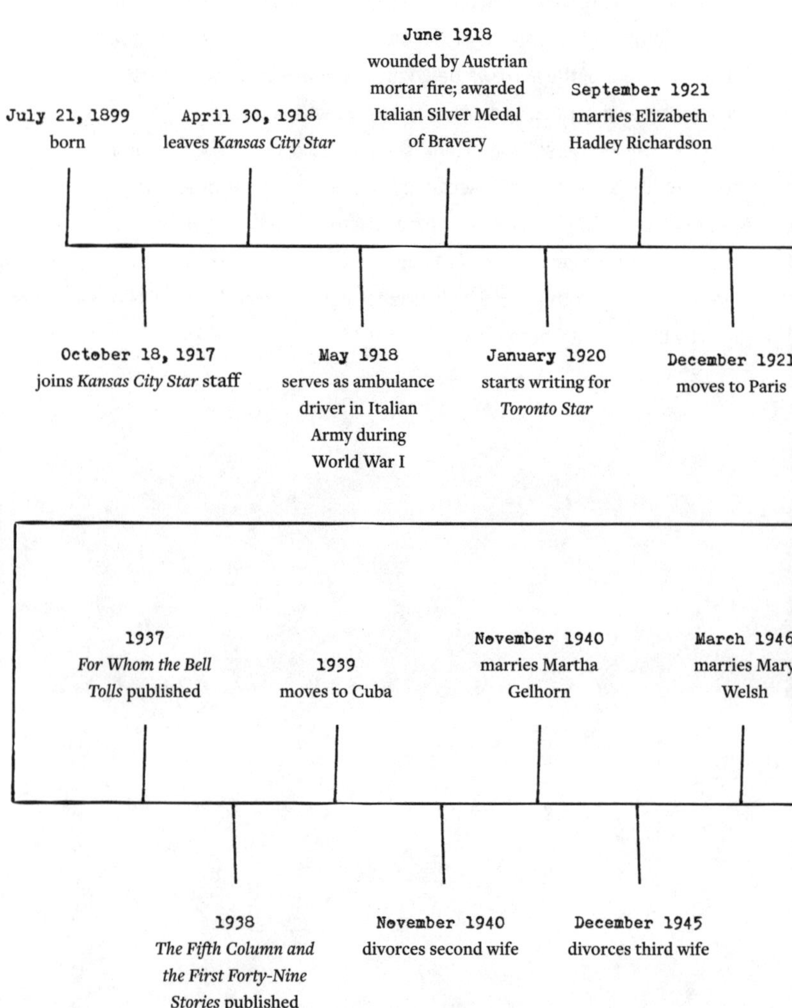

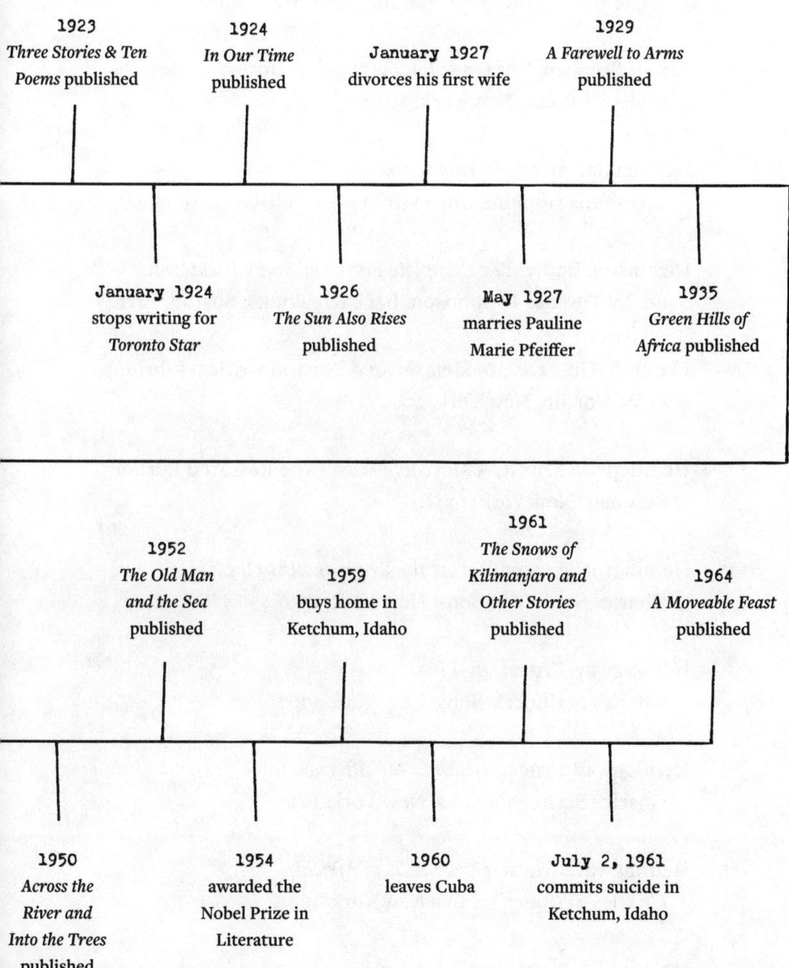
1923
Three Stories & Ten Poems published
1924
In Our Time published
January 1927
divorces his first wife
1929
A Farewell to Arms published
January 1924
stops writing for *Toronto Star*
1926
The Sun Also Rises published
May 1927
marries Pauline Marie Pfeiffer
1935
Green Hills of Africa published
1950
Across the River and Into the Trees published
1952
The Old Man and the Sea published
1954
awarded the Nobel Prize in Literature
1959
buys home in Ketchum, Idaho
1960
leaves Cuba
1961
The Snows of Kilimanjaro and Other Stories published
July 2, 1961
commits suicide in Ketchum, Idaho
1964
A Moveable Feast published

Bibliography

Brooks, Cleanth and Robert Penn Warren, Eds. *The Scope of Fiction.* Applenton-Century-Crofts, Inc.: New York. 1960.

Crane, Stephen. *The Open Boat and Other Stories.* Andecite Press: New York. 2017.

Derrida, Jacques. *Of Grammatology.* The Johns Hopkins University Press: Baltimore. 1998.

Dickinson, Emily. *The Complete Poems of Emily Dickinson.* Ed, by Thomas H. Johnson. Back Bay Books: Boston. 1976.

Flaubert, Gustave. *Madame Bovary* (Norton Critical Edition). W.W. Norton: New York. 2004.

Hemingway, Ernest. *A Moveable Feast* (The Restored Edition). Scribner: New York. 1964.

Hemingway, Ernest. *Across the River and Into the Trees.* Charles Scribner's Sons: New York. 1950.

Hemingway, Ernest. *By-Line.* Charles Scribner's Sons: New York. 1967.

Hemingway, Ernest. *Death in the Afternoon.* Charles Scribner's Sons: New York. 1932.

Hemingway, Ernest. *Green Hills of Africa.* Charles Scribner's Sons: New York. 1953.

Hemingway, Ernest. *Selected Letters - 1917-1961.*
Ed. by Carlos Baker. Scribner: New York. 1981.

Hemingway, Ernest. *The Complete Short Stories* (Finca Vigia Edition).
Scribner: New York. 1987.

Hemingway, Ernest. *The Old Man and the Sea.*
Scribner: New York. 1952.

Hemingway, Ernest. *The Sun Also Rises.*
Charles Scribner's Sons: New York. 1926.

Lynn, Kenneth S. *Hemingway.*
Simon and Schuster: New York. 1987.

Meyers, Jeffrey. *Hemingway: A Biography.*
Harper and Row, Publishers: New York. 1985.

Phillips, Larry W., Ed. *Ernest Hemingway on Writing.*
Scribner: New York. 1984.

Shipley, Joseph T. *Dictionary of World Literature.*
Littlefield, Adams and Co.: Totowa, New Jersey. 1972.

Stein, Gertrude. from *The Making of Americans.*
Munklinde Vestergaard: Berlin. 1994.

Tolstoy, Leo. *The Death of Ivan Ilych.*
Vintage Classics: New York. 2012.

Index

T

U

V

W

About the Author

E. J. Gleason taught American and Irish literatures at Saint Anselm College in Manchester, New Hampshire, for nearly half a century. A former chair of the English Department there, his published scholarship centered on the literary production of James Joyce, F. Scott Fitzgerald, John Updike, and the father/son fiction of Andre Dubus and Andre Dubus III. In his retirement, while continuing to take on various writing projects, he plays saxophone in a small jazz group and maintains a gallery of his fine art photography in his Durham, New Hampshire, home.

he Star Copy Style.

short sentences. Use short first
raphs. Use vigorous English. Be
ve, not negative.
style of local communications is
he *Star*: in italics, out-of-town
unications in this form. *Salina,*
-To The Star:
er use old slang. Such words as
cut out, got his goat, come across,
and take notice, put one over,
no place after their use becomes
on. Slang to be enjoyable must
esh.
Kas., not *Kan.* or *Kans.*, as an ab-
tion for Kansas; use *Ok.*, not
for Oklahoma, *Col.*, not *Colo.*, for
do; *Cal.*, not *Calif.*, for California.
your sequence of tenses. "He
he knew the truth, not "He *said*
ows the truth." "The community
mazed to hear that Charles Wake-
was a thief," not "*was amazed* to
that Charles Wakefield *is* a thief."
style of The Star is 9:30 *o'clock*
fternoon or *this morning* or *to-*
not 9:30 *this forenoon*, 9:30 *p.*
9:30 *this evening*. Also let the
precede—not *this morning at* 9:30
. He walked *twelve miles*, not *a*
ce of twelve miles; he *earned* $10,
earned *the amount* or *sum* of
e went there *to see his wife*, not
e purpose of seeing his wife. He
bsent *during June*, not *during the*
of June.
ds *valued at about* $25 were
" not "about $25 *worth of goods*
stolen."
eral fountain pens were stolen,"
number of fountain pens"—if
now the number, specify.
iminate every superfluous word as
ral services will be at 2 o'clock
y," not "*The* funeral services will

should like to see th
rected."
Don't say "He *had* h
an accident." He woul
done for anything.
"He *suffered* a broke
not "*he broke his leg*
didn't break the leg, the
leg, not his leg, because
man has two legs.
"The work *began*," no
begun."
"He *was graduated* fr
"*he graduated from* Me
Say Mary went shop
—not "*in company with*
"Honor *the memory*
Karnes" not "*honor* J
after his death,"
Say "John Jones of
comma between *Jones* a
"Mr Roosevelt is a
believe, would succeed,"
believe, would."
"Mr. Roosevelt is a h
believe the people w
"*who*, we believe."
"None saw him *excep*
saw him *but* me." Do
proposition.
Use *or* after *either*, n
as a general rule. Ce
from this statement ar
but extreme care in us
Indorsement of a ca
dorsement.
Say *Chinese*, not *Chi*
Bodies are not *shipp*
"The burial will be in
"Several *persons* wer
not "several *people*."
Kansas City" is correct
Both *persons* were pl
parties were pleased."
the contract" is correct
"He knew no good
should not run" is bet'e

About Cider Mill Press Book Publishers

Good ideas ripen with time. From seed to harvest, Cider Mill Press brings fine reading, information, and entertainment together between the covers of its creatively crafted books. Our Cider Mill bears fruit twice a year, publishing a new crop of titles each spring and fall.

"Where Good Books Are Ready for Press"

Visit us online at
cidermillpress.com
or write to us at
PO Box 454
12 Spring St.
Kennebunkport, Maine 04046